MAESTRO

SONGTELLER OF SAVANNAH VALLEY

RICK & STACIE FESSLER

MAESTRO : SONGTELLER OF SAVANNAH VALLEY

Quantity sales special discounts are available on quantity purchases by corporations, associations, and others. For details, contact the publisher at carol@markvictorhansenlibrary.com

Orders by U.S. trade bookstores and wholesalers.
Email: carol@markvictorhansenlibrary.com

Creative contribution by Jennifer Plaza.
Cover Design - Low & Joe Creative, Brea, CA 92821
Book Layout - DBree, StoneBear Design

Manufactured and printed in the United States of America distributed globally by markvictorhansenlibrary.com
Manufactured and printed in the United States of America distributed globally by markvictorhansenlibrary.com

MVHL

New York | Los Angeles | London | Sydney

ISBN: 979-8-88581-015-9 Hardback
ISBN: 979-8-88581-016-6 Paperback
ISBN: 979-8-88581-017-3 eBook
Library of Congress Control Number: 2022903655

THE SAVANNAH VALLEY SERIES

Everyone imagines what life will be like in retirement. Perhaps you know someone who ended up in a depressing nursing facility with people who didn't care about their health and wellbeing. That's not the way it has to be and that's not the way it is in Savannah Valley.

The characters in these books celebrate life and retirement in fun and imaginative ways after facing unexpected challenges. Here, new friendships are made, new horizons open, and a lifetime of experience and acquired wealth is celebrated.

Each book in the series is inspired by true events unique to each author. Sit back, relax, and allow yourself to be transported to the glorious and prestigious retirement community known as Savannah Valley.

Maestro : Songteller of Savannah Valley
by Rick & Stacie Fessler

All About Henry : Rich Widower of Savannah Valley
by Lyle Lee Jenkins

Love After : Dreams Still Come True
by Russell Gray & Mona Guarino

Nightingale : Say Goodbye to Yesterday
by Tony Lopes

Rich Widows of Savannah Valley
by Mitzi Perdue

Ruby : Magic Comes From the Heart
by Randall Kenneth Jones

markvictorhansenlibrary.com/savannah-valley

CONTENTS

ACKNOWLEDGMENTS

The death of Goddard's wife represents the end of a business I (Rick) spent almost half of my life building. To Stacie, the death of Maureen's husband represents the tragic loss of her mother.

The character Sydney represents Stacie's mother. She was never afraid to say what was on her mind, and she loved her dog (Riley – represented by Piazza) more than life itself.

The character Patrick represents Stacie's father Allen Rosen. Al is the one who taught Stacie what it looks like to play such an amazing, supportive role in a relationship.

The people speaking into me (Rick), saying that I had more to give after the sale of my business, are represented by the character Larry. A special thank you to the Larry's in my life—Ben McIntosh, John McCadden, Pastor Dion Garrett, and my incredible wife Stacie.

Goddard, being along in years and grieving the recent loss of the wife, his one true love, is reminiscent of Tom Hill, a mentor of mine whom I (Rick) admire and hope to be like some day.

Tom Hill, at the young age of 86, even after the loss of his beloved wife Betty, wakes up every day, gets in his car, and sets off to bless those in his life, and everyone he encounters along the way. Tom proves that you are never too old to live a life of purpose. Tom Hill is a Maestro, committed to bringing out the best in people. He is the one who challenged me to write my story. Thank you, Tom. I love you, and I will always do my best to make you proud.

The people who introduced me to and gave me the opportunity to explore my passion for entrepreneurship, are represented by the lady's choir that Goddard encountered at the community hall in New York City at that age of 14. A special thank you to my late uncle Carl Strieder, my late stepfather Steve Burris, and Rick and Cindy McKuin.

A special acknowledgement to my (Rick) parents, Rick and Peggy Fessler, and Kathy Burris. They have always believed in me and have supported anything I have ever wanted to do.

I (Stacie) would like to acknowledge my aunt and uncle, Geoff and Leeti Temple, for always being there for me through every season of my life.

Stacie and I would not be where we are today without our Faith. A special thank you to those who have shown and taught us what it looks like to walk in Faith, knowing God is always by your side . . . no matter your situation or circumstance. Thank you to Tim and Chandra Fessler, Ben and Natalie McIntosh, Jae Chung, Pastors' Dion Garrett, and Stephen Hower. Without all of you constantly exemplifying what it looks like to live a life of Faith, Stacie and I may have lost our way...and our lives would look completely different today.

DEDICATIONS

Finally, Stacie and I would like to dedicate this book to a man that is and forever will be a Maestro, Chris Toomey. Chris taught so many of us what it looks like to live life with a heart of a Maestro. He lived his life dedicated to the success of others. He saw the best in people and poured into everyone. If given the chance to live out his life here on earth, we have no doubt he would have been the Maestro of Maestros'. Rest in peace our friend, you are missed.

PROLOGUE

Imagine walking into a concert hall and hearing individual instruments warming up on their own. It would sound like chaos. Suddenly someone dressed in a perfectly pressed, perfectly tailored tuxedo appears. With the raise of a baton, silence. Musicians' eyes are now locked on the Maestro, awaiting their cue. As he or she gently waves the baton with one hand, gracefully gesturing with the other, an amazing sound engulfs your soul. What was once chaos, is now a symphony of talents all playing for the same outcome . . . a concert worthy of your time and money. A symphony that will leave you wanting more.

The life of a Maestro is not easy. You spend a lifetime studying the great artists who came before you. You envision the kind of music you want to create. Then, you have to convince a hundred other individuals—from different backgrounds, skills, and stories—to see and hear what you see and hear. You need to believe in them, even if they don't believe in themselves. Then, you must call on them, individually or in sections, to recreate that vision.

To accomplish this feat with any success, you must know and understand music at a level most of us may never comprehend. But it's also important to be able to see in people what they might not see in themselves. You need to connect with people on a level that is so attuned, that both you and they have the confidence to arrive at your vision. Only then can you create a masterful concerto together. A maestro's ability to inspire a group of musicians to perform at a level they themselves may not believe possible is their true hidden talent.

What if you were a maestro? What if you inspired others to achieve what they didn't believe possible? What would the world be like, if we all behaved like maestros, tuning in to the hearts of others, inspiring them to realize their hopes and dreams?

In the following chapters, you will meet a man who gave hope and possibilities to those he encountered, even from a young age. He turned his passion for music—and his hunger to inspire excellence in others—into a world-renowned career. After tragedy struck, he believed that his professional life had come to an end. But his passions took a surprising new turn, renewing his purpose and those of the people around him.

CHAPTER ONE

Louis XIII

oddard clutched the black-velvet bag to his chest as he approached the doorman stationed in front of his new condominium building in Savannah Valley. The young man's spotless white gloves and the brass buttons on his red uniform jacket reminded Goddard of the good old days, when he played the clubs in New York, Chicago, and Los Angeles. Back then, those brass buttons were an unspoken sign of a high-class establishment, where patrons could escape bustling pedestrians and chaotic car horns. Expecting his new home to offer a similar refuge, he locked eyes with the attendant, a silent directive that said, "Follow me."

The attendant used the bell cart to load the newcomer's luggage: a trunk filled with unfinished compositions and manuscripts, two suitcases with foldable clothes, and on top of the secured suitcases, a small, silver, locked case. Goddard watched the man steer the brass cart through the glass doors and across the lobby, until he stopped beside the elevator. Satisfied, Goddard made his way to the white-marble counter to register. The young woman sitting at the computer was chewing her lip in concentration and didn't notice him at first. Goddard cleared his throat, and she looked up and smiled.

"Good afternoon, sir. Welcome to Savannah Valley," the woman chimed. "May I have your name, please?"

"Goddard Sampson," he replied in an even, controlled voice, the kind of voice one chose for personal business. Not unkind, but just sharp enough to deter any unwanted conversation. He was retired and looked forward to peace and tranquility, something the big city scene did not afford.

The woman kept smiling. "Here is your private key card, Mr. Sampson. Your penthouse is on the ninth floor. If you need anything at all, please let me know." She handed the card to Goddard and then took a brochure from a drawer beneath her desk. "The amenities are listed on the back, and inside is a map of the facility."

Goddard took the key card but shook his head no to the brochure. Amenities didn't interest him. The point of retirement is to relax, reflect, and relish the time one has left, he thought. Preferably, over a sipping brandy. That last thought caused the corner of his mouth to tug upward. He turned toward the mahogany elevator doors and nodded to the doorman. The young man's white-gloved finger pressed the keypad for "nine" and the door opened. Goddard stepped in, and the man followed with the loaded cart.

The doors of the neighboring elevator opened. A silver-haired woman in a mauve tracksuit rushed off, carrying a fluffy, white dog under her arm. Her rose-pink lipstick reminded him of the carpet at Carnegie Hall, one of many memories that resurfaced without warning. Clutching his velvet bag tighter, he stood in the corner of the elevator beside the cart and stared at the number line atop the door. Thankfully, there was no elevator music. The attendant stood at attention, silent as well.

Retirement is good, Goddard told himself.

The elevator gave a soft "ding" when they reached the ninth floor. The doors whispered open and Goddard stood in the glossy elevator box, taking in the penthouse's marble salon with his beloved Steinway beneath a crystal chandelier. He hoped the moving company had delivered his belongings safe and sound prior to his arrival. He had arranged for them to set up the flat.

The attendant motioned for Goddard to proceed first, then he followed, wheeling the cart onto the royal-blue carpet. "Where would you like your bags, Mr. Sampson?" He did not cast his eyes down when Goddard looked at him.

Goddard pointed to an empty space beneath a large gold-leaf-trimmed mirror. He waited by the door for the attendant to leave and slipped him a twenty-dollar bill before the elevator door closed.

Goddard leaned against the white-marble wall trimmed in gold and removed a jade vase from the velvet bag he was still clutching. "We're home, Allie-Kat." He set his wife's urn on the mahogany Steinway and pulled the silver case from the stack. Then he settled into one of the two Chippendale wingback chairs he'd had sent from his penthouse in New York. He pulled a key from his jacket pocket, balanced the case in his lap, and unlocked the lid. The Baccarat metal flask glistened in the sunlit room. It was a retirement gift he'd purchased for himself; a cognac fit for a French king.

He set the bottle on the glass end table and found a Triton crystal snifter on a black, marble-topped bar in the corner of the salon. He returned to his chair and poured the cognac into the glass, a quarter full.

"Siri, play Rossini's *Bassoon Concerto 1*." The silence of his transition ended. Music emanated from the Cabasse speakers. Goddard sank into his chair and sipped the cognac, lost in the lilting bassoon solo. The Rossini crescendo began, each repeated phrase a tad louder than the one before. The peak forced a smile from his lips and made him open his eyes, swirl his brandy, and prepare for another rich, fruity sip. But in the height of the crescendo, a grating buzz stopped him mid-swirl. A yellow light flashed on the video panel by the elevator door.

Now what? he wondered. He wasn't in the mood for company. All he wanted was a respite from the grueling flight from Los Angeles to Savannah, a flight that should have taken five hours but took twenty due to fog and a layover in Chicago. It was one of those rare times when

Goddard wished he had just chartered a plane. He set the glass down and shuffled to the door. "Yes?" He peered at the screen.

The rose-lipped tenant waved in the camera, sans the fluffy dog. "Welcome committee!"

Oh great, Goddard thought glumly. But he couldn't just send them away and get a reputation as a curmudgeon (even though he was fast becoming one). He pressed the button to allow access and stood by the elevator door, his hands tucked in the pockets of his slacks. The whoosh of the elevator settled, the doors slid open, and not one, but three women, dressed in Bottega Veneta jumpsuits, stood before him. He recognized the Italian designer, because it had been one of his wife's favorites.

One of the women—slender, with silver hair pulled into a high ponytail and a sun-kissed complexion—held a bottle of Dom Perignon P3 Plenitude Brut. "Good afternoon, I'm Sydney David, chairperson of the welcome committee. And this is Linda Foss." She pulled the leggy redhead to her side.

Linda stepped forward, a cheery smile spread across her face. "I make it my business to know all the new faces in Savannah Flats condos. I live on the second floor, next to Sydney and Maureen Maxwell." She gestured to the third woman.

Maureen held a single yellow rose. She sported a pony-tail, too, but her hair was black and her lips were covered with a dewy gloss that brought out the deep merlot, her natural lip color. Her hazel eyes focused on Goddard's gold, treble-clef cufflinks. "I like music too," she said, handing him the rose and nudging Sydney to remind her that she still held the champagne. Sydney handed him the bottle.

Goddard accepted the gift and stepped aside for them to enter. "Thank you, ladies."

Maureen stood between Sydney and Linda. She extended her hand to Goddard and met his gaze. "Welcome, Mr. Sampson. I'm a newcomer, too. I just moved in two weeks ago." Goddard noticed she wore a tennis bracelet on her slender wrist that matched her diamond-stud earrings. He also noticed how she looked at him with interest. He knew women called him a "silver fox" because of his white hair and beard, and it amused him. But he wasn't interested in dating, maybe never would be. His eyes drifted to his wife's urn on top of the piano. Right then, he missed her so much, it felt like a knife in his heart.

Maureen raised one eyebrow before stepping back for her counterparts to have their go. Goddard gave each woman's hand a gentle squeeze. He knew they meant well, but he was exhausted after his long trip. "I didn't expect to have a welcome party on day one," he admitted, "but please, have a seat." He gestured toward the camelback needlepoint sofa facing the Chippendale chairs.

The women made themselves comfortable, while

Goddard took the Dom to the bar and retrieved four champagne flutes. "Siri, volume 3," he ordered, and the concerto's volume diminished. He found a corkscrew and opened the bottle with a pop. Then he caught the foaming liquid in his glass as the cork skidded across the white marble floor. He poured the champagne and handed each woman a flute. "To new acquaintances."

Sydney held her glass a bit higher. "Nay, to new friends."

"I'll second that," Linda said. "Salut."

They raised their glasses and sipped.

Maureen sat in the Chippendale chair beside the one Goddard had occupied moments before. She nodded at the cognac and metal decanter. "Is that . . . Louis XIII? There are only 300 available. Who'd you have to kill to get one?"

Goddard gave an enigmatic smile. "You really want to know?"

CHAPTER TWO

Welcome Committee

$\mathcal{M}$aureen laughed. "You're joking."

"Am I?" Goddard said, lifting one eyebrow.

Sydney and Maureen exchanged a nervous glance.

Linda tapped Goddard's arm and let out a forced laugh. "Oh, you. You remind me of my Adam. He was always pulling someone's leg." She sipped her champagne. "Seriously, Mr. Sampson, we did our homework, I assure you. You are, of course, *the* Goddard Sampson."

Sydney blinked at her new neighbor's now-serious face. "Linda, there was nothing disclosed in Maureen's briefing during our brunch at Sky." She turned to Goddard. "That's the restaurant on the top floor of the Tower building, the highest point in Savannah Valley." She turned back to Linda. "That was three days before we scheduled Mr. Sampson's welcoming." She swiveled back to Goddard. "Maureen emailed a list of ten hyperlinks to both Linda and me, in the name of research. It's her duty to stay on top of the 'who's who' game."

Maureen sipped her champagne. "Sydney and Linda depend on my digging skills," she said, chuckling. She leaned into Goddard, taking over the big reveal. "Yes, you were just twelve years old when you gave your first piano concert with an original work. At age nineteen, you were drafted into the army, then came home and studied music at Yale. Afterward, you travelled to Stockholm to study at the Royal College of Music. From there, you toured the world as a piano virtuoso, until you fell in love with the art of conducting. You developed a technique to ensure your own compositions would be performed exactly as you intended. Then Hollywood offered you a way to use all your talents, composing and directing movie soundtracks. Although, you still accepted positions as a guest conductor throughout your career. You finally decided to retire at age 74, a year after . . ." Her voice dropped to a whisper. "A year after your wife's passing. I'm so sorry for your loss."

Goddard nodded. "Go on."

Linda nodded back and took a sip of champagne. "In your last interview, you stated that all acts must come to an end, and it was time for your curtain to close. I'm a huge fan, Mr. Sampson. Your words were poetic and summed up what many of us feel. We live our lives striving to achieve, but then the curtains draw closed. I'm truly sorry for your loss."

Goddard put his champagne flute on the glass side table, picked up his snifter with the amber King Louis XIII cognac, and sipped. "Ladies, I am at a disadvantage. You know all about me."

Sydney smiled, "Well, to be fair, Maestro, you *are* a bit of a celebrity."

Goddard nodded. "Touché. But please, don't call me Maestro, those days are over. Call me Goddard. Anyway, enough about me. What brought you ladies to Savannah Valley?" He wrinkled his forehead and drew his brows together, signaling he was intrigued.

Maureen focused on Goddard's face and cocked her head. "That's the same look my agent gives me when I submit an outline for a new novel." Goddard nodded in encouragement, and Maureen continued, but first, she took a sip of the bubbling liquid in her crystal flute. "I came here to find tranquility, make some new friends, and come up with a plan to end my book series. To pull the curtain closed on my writing career and start a new life." She wiggled her flute at Sydney who had taken possession of the bottle of Dom and poured her half a glass. "Never in my wildest dreams did I imagine saying 'yes' when the realtor wanted to show me a flat here in Savannah Valley." She laughed. "I never believed I'd live someplace not on the ground that cost three million dollars."

Linda and Sydney chuckled. Goddard wondered if, like him, they'd both lived in luxury New York City properties in the sky—and therefore found nothing unbelievable about it.

Maureen continued. "I guess you figured out I'm a writer. The *Inspector Webster* series?" She gave a self-conscious smile. "Although I doubt they'd be your cup of tea."

"They absolutely are!" Goddard said. "I've read a few of your books, Maureen. A talent like yours should not be put to rest." He gave her a reassuring smile.

Maureen beamed. "Thank you. As it turns out, I've decided to continue my detective series, and I even have plans for another. When I moved here, I was overwhelmed with life. But this place takes care of everything. I can sit back, relax, and not think about everyday qualms. Just concentrate on my writing. I was lonely before, too." She laughed. "Imagine that—an award-winning novelist with books published in thirty-six countries was lonely."

"Well, I'm glad Savannah Valley reignited your spark," Goddard said, lifting his glass in a salute.

"Thank you," Maureen answered, her cheeks flushing.

Sydney squeezed her shoulder. "What happened to your husband?"

"I lost Frank twelve years ago. He was an insurance broker who also dabbled in wealth management and investments. On a business trip to Oregon, his plane went down. There were three on board—no survivors." Maureen gulped the rest of her champagne.

Linda patted Maureen's arm. "Sydney, how about you?" Linda rerouted the conversation to keep the welcoming cheerful. "Tell us how you and your husband ended up here."

Sydney rose from the couch and wandered to the

floor-to-ceiling windows that offered a panoramic view of the lake and golf course. She gazed out for a moment, then turned and began her story. "Funny, a few months back, my husband Patrick and I saw an ad for Savannah Valley while driving to Key West. I wanted to peek at the new construction, and he was all for a stop. I called for a tour, and we met with one of the new owners, Darcy. She was a fireball. She told me this place was opened by swindlers, and when they were ousted, she and two friends jumped on the business opportunity. We took an instant liking to her and were intrigued by the history, especially the infamous *three rich widows.* "

Sydney sipped her champagne and paced in front of the windows. "This place is the most expensive and exclusive retirement community in the country. It's set on three thousand acres with four hundred homes, as well as this new ten-story condominium building, Savannah Flats. Wow, I sound like a real estate agent! But I love this place so much, and so does my husband. Right now, he's out playing eighteen holes of golf , and afterward, we're going to dinner at Sky."

Goddard considered clapping but smiled and sipped his cognac instead. He stole a glance at his watch. He'd wanted solitude, time to reflect on whatever it was people reflected on. But the three women had made themselves at home in his salon and showed no signs of leaving. In spite of himself, he gave a deep sigh. The women noticed and exchanged "time to go" looks. "I know, such a bore, aren't I?," Sydney said, walking to the bar and placing her empty glass on top. "Tell you what. You get settled, Mr. Sampson. We all have dinner reservations for seven o'clock. If you feel like company, please join us."

"Thank you, but that's not necessary." Goddard tried to get the point across, without being rude. He stood in hopes of them following his direction.

"From what I understand, there's a performance tonight," Linda murmured.

Goddard couldn't help himself. "A performance, you say?"

Maureen stood and placed her hand on his arm. "Do I detect an ember of interest smoldering?"

Goddard, being a man who thinks a lot but says little, smiled. He'd hung up his baton and wanted to rest, but the performance intrigued him. "On second thought, I *will* break bread with you and yours, this evening at seven." He glanced at his watch again. "Oh, look at the time. I won't keep you further. You've all taken too much of your time for me already."

Sydney motioned for the other two women to stand beside her. She collected their glasses and set them on the bar. Then she clasped Goddard's forearm. "We'll leave you for now, Mr. Sampson."

Goddard pressed the elevator button for the three women and bowed his head.

"See you tonight!" Linda called, her voice higher than it had been before.

Goddard nodded, a folded lip smile in place. "Seven."

"If you need anything, just ring. Here's my card." Sydney handed him her business card. "I can't wait for Patrick to meet you."

Goddard closed his eyes and nodded a little faster.

"We'll get out of your hair now, bye." Maureen fluttered her fingers and hurried onto the elevator with her two friends.

Goddard waved to the women as the elevator doors squeezed shut.

CHAPTER THREE

Breaking Bread

The grandfather clock in Goddard's salon chimed. He stepped inside from his balcony, where he'd been observing the duffers on the tenth hole, and began counting with each repetition. "One, two, three, four, five, six," he said, wielding an imaginary baton. "Hmmm, "Dinner Adagio in E Major." He chuckled to himself. The last time he'd jested about a concerto, it had given him the idea for an award-winning soundtrack.

The silence in his penthouse was unsettling. Goddard was a man of music, but hadn't he yearned for peace and quiet and time to reflect? So reflect he did, sinking into his favorite wingback chair and recalling how his music career began. He was only fourteen years old . . .

***

"Ladies," Mrs. Planket called, clapping her hands to get the chattering under control. Their rendition of "Give My Regards to Broadway," by George M. Cohan, captured young Goddard's attention. Anything Broadway or show-biz brought a twinkle to his eye. He stopped in the doorway to community hall and observed the women in the chorus trying to match their pitches to the woman standing before them. But each time she hummed, it was a slight bit off.

To the untrained ear it sounded fine, but to Goddard, the sound sent a shiver up his spine like nails on a chalkboard. He'd been afforded the opportunity to learn music and was in a position to share his knowledge. He knew every ear could be trained with proper guidance. When the singers left their spaces for a lemonade break, the teenager made his way to the woman in charge.

"Excuse me, ma'am," he said. He held his chin straight and looked her in the eye with confidence, just as his music teacher had taught him. She said it showed respect without cowardice.

The woman stared at him. "What are you doing here, boy?"

"I heard your music from the street." He glanced around and saw there was no pianist. "Mind if I play for you?"

The singers gathered behind the stern woman. "Go on, Mrs. Planket. Let's see what the boy can do."

Mrs. Planket frowned at Goddard. "We're performing in two weeks. I do not have time for curious boys."

"Please," one of the younger singers urged, "our music brought him in. How can we turn him away?"

An older singer chimed in, "We're on a break anyway, let's see what he's got." She sipped her lemonade and bit a cookie.

"Okay, make it quick," Mrs. Planket said, still frowning.

Goddard nodded in anticipation. He took a seat at the worn upright piano and played a series of double-octave scales before pulling the original Cohan tune from the recesses of his youthful mind. His limber fingers danced over the keys. He played around with the melody, bringing it up an octave and ending on a high note.

The women applauded. So did Mrs. Planket, although her face was still stern, as if she needed more proof of his talent.

"If you'll have me, I can play for you. It can give you a point of reference when you practice. There isn't anything I can't play," Goddard gushed.

The women grew silent. Mrs. Planket turned to Goddard. "The reason we do not have an accompanist is because we can't afford to pay."

"I don't want money. I just want to help."

From that point forward, until he was drafted into the army at nineteen, Goddard played for the women on the Upper East Side. He never earned a nickel, but he acquired an education unlike any given in a proper institution. His community outreach touched over a hundred lives, both young and old. And each of those lives would make their appearance later in his career, through instrumental interludes and passages. Even then, he knew that every life was music, a melody to be explored.

***

If not for that first experience, Goddard mused, he wouldn't be where he was today, standing in front of a gilded mirror dressed in an Armani tailored suit and starched white shirt. After more than fifty years enticing audiences from the podium, he was making his debut tonight at Savannah Valley. He tucked a pocket watch in his vest and straightened his bow tie. This was his ritual, no matter the performance, and in life, every day was a performance. The face he put on for the welcome committee women, the doorman, or even for his beloved wife, were all sides of a man filling different roles.

The world was filled with actors, and Goddard was a skilled performer. He tucked a handkerchief into his jacket pocket as he considered the evening ahead. Three ladies, intent on making his first evening enjoyable, while taking the sting out of being new and alone, awaited his arrival. He flashed a smile in the mirror. Time to put on his public face.

***

Goddard stood outside the glass elevator's door on the Tower's lower level. The Sky restaurant was at the top, along with his female entourage and one husband. He smiled at the thought of the poor man being brought into the awkward meeting. Goddard remembered how his wife had been the one to endure function after function, meeting after meeting. She wore gowns and pantsuits, shook hands, and often kissed the cheeks of people she barely knew. And yet, she was still better at conversation than he was. He sighed, "Well, it's my turn now, Alli-Kat."

The doorman set the elevator to the sixth floor. Goddard stood alone in the glass cylinder and watched the curb shrink below. He turned when the doors dinged. The expansive restaurant lay before him. He stepped out onto a black granite floor polished to a mirror finish. Floor-to-ceiling windows presented a 360-degree view of Savannah Valley. Folding glass doors opened to an outside dining area providing an unobstructed view and a continuation of the ebony wood tables dressed in snowy white linens. The host, clad in a black tuxedo, approached him.

"Welcome to Sky in the Tower," he said, giving a half-bow. "My name is Arthur. Will you be dining alone this evening?"

Goddard scanned the expanse and saw Maureen wave at him from across the room. "Actually, no. My party is already here."

Arthur turned to see Sydney and Linda joining Maureen. "Very well, if you'll follow me, sir, I will take you to your party."

Goddard clasped his hands behind him and followed the host. He noticed many of the tables had singletons. Some people had laptops; others sipped wine while scrolling on their phones. A few other tables were full, but where he was headed had been turned into a table for six.

Maureen stood to greet him. The novelist wore a navy sequined gown with matching flats. Sydney sat across from her in a white skirt suit. She attempted to rise after seeing Maureen, but Goddard held his palm up. With a slight nod and a wink, he let her know it wasn't necessary, but the effort was appreciated. Her husband, Patrick, rose and shook Goddard's hand.

"A man who takes his golf seriously, I like it," Goddard joked, commenting on Patrick's maroon polo with the NIKE logo and black golf slacks.

"Do you play?" Patrick asked, sitting back down. "Not for years, and nothing serious," Goddard admitted.

"We'll have to coordinate a tee time once you're settled. Are you free on Friday?"

Sydney jabbed her elbow into Patrick's arm. "Please excuse my husband; he does get excited about the course here."

Linda, clad in a simple-but-elegant black linen dress and pearls, sipped her white wine and rolled her eyes. "Allow me to make a proper introduction. Goddard, this is Sydney's husband Patrick. Patrick, this is *the* Goddard Sampson." She motioned for the newcomer to sit between her and Maureen.

"The view this evening is lovely," Sydney declared, turning to Goddard. "I'm so glad you agreed to join us." She motioned to the waiter by wiggling her wine glass, and the young man hurried over. "And what will you be drinking this evening, sir?" he asked Goddard.

"Pinot noir, please."

The waiter left to fetch the wine. Goddard was certain whatever came would be more than adequate. He might be particular about his brandy, but he wasn't a wine snob. He was on team red for all meals, whether he was eating seafood or beef. He felt wine was like fine art. Either you liked it, or you didn't.

"Wait until you see the menu! They have black, farm-raised caviar over crème fraiche on crisps, paired with a Bloody Mary shrimp cocktail," Linda cooed. "I just love a loaded Bloody Mary. It's like one of those milkshakes with a heap of toppings, but for adults."

Maureen lifted her eyebrows. "Then I guess I'm in my second childhood, because I just love those milkshakes. Especially the ones with bacon and peanut butter!" She glanced at the menu. "I'll get my usual, the grilled pear salad and smoked salmon."

Sydney sighed, "I should get the salad, too, but I really want that Bloody Mary. Would it be tacky if we had two orders the same?" She bit her lip. "Linda, you wouldn't mind, would you?"

"Sure, why the hell not," Patrick said. "And the bone-in rib eye."

Linda waved her hand for the waiter to come back and

the five placed their orders. Maureen wound up adding a Bloody Mary to her order, too. When the waiter returned with the five cocktails, the three women clapped.

Patrick sat straight and raised his brow, impressed. "Not what I expected at all. That's fantastic."

"Wait, I want a picture." Maureen took her phone out of her clutch purse and shot several photos from different angles. She made sure to get the shrimp skewer, celery stalk, bacon strip, pickled egg, batter fried octopus, and olive strip. "It's a meal in a glass. I love it."

"You could use it for inspiration in one of your books ," Goddard suggested. "A cocktail of this magnitude deserves a mention."

Maureen blushed and put her phone back in her clutch.

"Toast!" Sydney announced and raised her Bloody Mary, balancing the drink's overloaded glass. "To Goddard, new friends, and Savannah Valley for bringing us together."

The five did an air clink to avoid dropping their garnishes. Patrick pulled the shrimp skewer out and bit off the shrimp, one by one. "This is some pretty good shrimp. Reminds me of working on the docks of New York back in my school days. The fish market. That was some fresh stuff."

"Sydney mentioned you happened to stop here on your

way to Key West. What made you consider settling here?" Goddard asked. He had a genuine curiosity, because the man reminded him of his good buddy Larry. "What line of business were you in?"

Patrick wiped his lips with the white linen napkin. "Dough."

Sydney bit the alcohol-rich end of her celery stalk and rolled it to the inner part of her cheek. "Frozen bread, to be precise. We supply grocery store bakeries across the country with frozen dough to bake fresh on site. Patrick took over the company from his parents when they retired to Boca. We always thought we'd follow in their footsteps but found this place and fell in love. We can still travel, but why bother? There's so much to do here, at least for the present." She chewed the celery and then sipped the iced beverage. "I like a good cruise, so there may be that in the future."

"Interesting. Food is always needed. Good niche. Well, congratulations on your retirement and new life," Goddard said. He sipped his own beverage, fearing his conversational skills were subpar. As a musician, he could express his emotions and say what he wanted without using words. As a composer, he could weave a story with depth through mere notes on a staff. And as a conductor, he need only look at his orchestra and he was understood. He'd depended on his wife to get him through social engagements, because she could talk to anyone. He sighed. "And you, Linda? I don't believe you said what your line of business involved." He hoped he didn't sound too formal. He gulped the Bloody Mary and nibbled an olive off its skewer.

"Oh, I guess I didn't mention it," Linda said. "I started a wealth-management firm for small businesses with as little as $25,000 in investible assets. Usually, financial services focus on the wealthy and ultra-wealthy, but there are small businesses that can use the guidance to grow their wealth. When they do, they provide for their communities through jobs, grants, donations, and such. I created a franchise that seemed to fill a niche, as you put it, and amassed my own fortune through franchising. We cover everything from tax planning to legal guidance. It's affordable and gives the smaller communities a professional service that is a small-scale model of what the big guys do."

Goddard sat back, "Wow. That's smart. I never would have given wealth management a thought if my wife, Alice-Katherine, hadn't opened my eyes. I had all this money sitting in the bank and had no clue what to do with it. Sometimes, when you're playing clubs and traveling, you forget you're getting paid the amount you do. You eat a burger and fries or hot pastrami and crash in a local hotel room. Maybe get comped a night. Then you become someone, I wouldn't say famous, but . . . anyway, then you get comped because of who you are, and there are royalties, which opens the door for people to take advantage of you. My Allie-Kat was always on the ball." He smiled and sipped the Bloody Mary through the paper straw.

"Hey, this looks like a fun table." A tall woman with a silver evening gown strode up to Goddard's side. "My name is Edith. I'm one of the owners here at Savannah Valley. I wanted to personally welcome you, Maestro Goddard Sampson. We try to reach out to all our new neighbors."

"Well, thank you," Goddard said, dabbing his napkin to his lips. He pushed out his chair, took her hand and kissed the back. "I am delighted to make your acquaintance. But please, just call me Goddard. My maestro days are over."

"Of course. The pleasure is all mine. I just love your work." She looked over the table. "I have to get me one of those cocktails tonight. They look delicious. I wanted to make myself seen and let you know that we're here for you. I do hope you enjoy yourselves."

As she spoke, the waiter arrived with two others helping to carry the five caviar samplers and Patrick's entree. A young man in a tuxedo started to play light jazz on the piano, and the lights dimmed. Faux candles glowed in the table centerpieces.

"This is gorgeous, I love the ambiance," Maureen said to Edith.

"I'm glad you like it. And Mr. Goddard, I do hope you enjoy Savannah Valley's own talents." Edith smiled and waved to the group before heading to another table near the folding glass doors.

Patrick started in on his rib eye, while Goddard continued to eat the shrimp on his cocktail. The jazz warmed him. He realized that his soul missed the music. He'd been on edge, and the piano soothed his heart and calmed his mind. He settled back in his chair and smiled at his new friends.

"I was thinking," Linda said, "that perhaps we could get a few other people from the building together. You know, like a soirée."

"That's a great idea," Maureen agreed. "Goddard should know who's who."

He snapped back to the moment. "What are we talking about?"

"I think tomorrow, what do you say?"

"I guess that's fine,' he said without thinking. "But what, exactly, are we talking about?"

"They want you to meet the people in our building tomorrow," Patrick explained, mid chew. "Probably at your place."

"Oh, okay." Goddard flushed. What had he just agreed to?

"Yay! I'll contact everyone. How is nine o'clock?" Sydney asked.

Goddard put his skewer on his plate and raised his eyebrows at Patrick. "Should be fine."

Patrick gave a rueful smile, shaking his head.

Linda raised her half-empty Bloody Mary, "Then here's to more new friends!"

CHAPTER FOUR

Curtains

ive couples, and enough single women to make the party count an even thirty, filled Goddard's salon. He had arranged for a caterer to take charge of the refreshments. Entertaining wasn't something he enjoyed doing, but the women had decided to have a shindig. Without his actual consent. At his penthouse.

Before the party, he moved Alice's urn from the piano to his bedroom and placed it on the window ledge over-looking the lake. She'd loved water, be it an ocean or a stream; it brought the smile he adored to her face. Now she would share the incredible view with him.

The caterers arrived an hour early to set up in the bar and kitchen areas. The Savannah Valley community had them on retainer. Rolling cases of finished canapes and hors d'oeuvres were parked next to the floor-to-ceiling windows in the salon. A sushi chef opened a wooden table on top of a black-marble-looking cooler. He prepared several California rolls before slicing into a deep-red tuna fillet.

As nine o'clock chimed on the grandfather clock, the yellow light lit up the pad by the elevator door. It was the

46 | RICK & STACIE FESSLER

doorman with the first guests. Goddard had instructed him to bring them up as they arrived.

Murmurs and laughter started the moment they stepped off the elevator. The smartly dressed group included residents of the building, but the welcome committee had told Goddard to expect some people from other parts of the community, as well. He shook hands, learned names (and then forgot them), made small talk, and graciously accepted compliments on his penthouse.

As he circulated, he noticed a woman wearing a fringed shawl sitting alone. She was drinking what appeared to be cola and nibbling cheese and crackers from a small plate. No alcohol, no fancy food. He watched as she absorbed her surroundings. An observer and "absorber" himself, he recognized the look. All five senses were at work. Then she stood and carried her glass and plate into the adjoining room and placed them on the glass tabletop next to a pink-velvet wingback chair.

Just that morning, Goddard had designated it the "entertaining room." It contained a smaller version of the piano in the salon. The room itself was a spacious 1,000 square feet, and besides the piano, the only furnishings were two wingback chairs with a glass cocktail table between them. The woman floated to the piano and exposed the keyboard. Goddard watched her scan the keys while he sipped his brandy—not the Louis, for that was an indulgence to be experienced alone.

The woman sat at the piano and let her fingers float over the keys in a gentle crescendo then she started to sing, "Fly me to the moon . . ." Her voice was strong and unafraid, but restrained. The music became a part of her as she closed her eyes and hummed to the melody, leaning into the chorus. The room silenced as the guests turned to watch.

***

Goddard was taken back to The Red Room, a bar in Manhattan's Lower East Side. It was late, and rain pelted the pedestrians as they scurried down the sidewalks, seeking shelter and a drink. He was no exception.

The bar was painted black on the outside and easy to miss if you didn't know the place. He pushed through the heavy metal door and entered the smoke-filled room with its red-velvet seats, shellacked tabletops, and carpeted walls. He spied his friend, Larry Winfield, seated at the bar. The big man had a half-full bottle of rye in front of him and was busy drowning in liquor.

Goddard headed straight for him. It was his custom to unwind at the end of the day by ducking into the old speakeasy turned dive. He removed his wet trench coat and hat, placing them on a stool beside Larry. A lifted finger signaled to Bob, the bartender, he wanted his own serving of liquid gold. The man nodded and placed a gin and tonic before him.

"That's a ladies' drink," Larry teased.

"So be it," Goddard grinned. He slicked back his thick, black locks, leaned on the bar, and sipped. Larry was a war buddy, someone he'd been lucky enough to ride next to on the plane home from Nam, both of them dressed in army fatigues and hiding scarred hearts. Larry was in the city on business and had said he needed Goddard's assistance. "What do you need me to do?" Goddard asked.

Larry laughed. "You make it sound all gangster'."

"Is it?"

Larry shook his head. The piano on the small stage came to life. It was background noise, something to fill the air with more than drunken banter and bartering. "I'm offering you a job."

Goddard studied his glass and sipped. "Yeah?"

"Yup."

Goddard nodded.

The piano music grew louder, an intro. A few notes and then, "Blow me a kiss . . ." wrapped the room with a voice to rival Kitty Kallen herself.

Goddard's attention was no longer focused on Larry. It had shifted to the brown-haired beauty, in a red, sequined dress, owning the stage.

Larry turned full around to take in the young woman.

"Alice Katherine. She's new. Bob says she's a shy farm girl from upstate."

"Shhh," Goddard said.

Larry shook his head.

The woman stood next to the baby grand. Her red-gloved hand ran along the edge. She stepped up to the microphone, eyes closed, and captivated the room with her mezzo-soprano rendition of *Little Things Mean A Lot*.

Goddard glanced at Larry. "I'm going to marry that voice."

Larry swallowed the contents of his glass and returned his gaze back to the bar. "Good luck, Keys."

Keys was the nickname Larry gave Goddard in their army days, because the young musician would find a piano at a local bar and start playing Tin Pan Alley songs. They were upbeat, fun pieces, the opposite of what they had to endure. Larry was from Los Angeles and hell bent on becoming a producer. His father was already in the business. Goddard had less lofty aspirations. He wanted a gig playing piano for places like The Red Room. Little did he know how much their roles would reverse.

Goddard ended up in Hollywood as a conductor, while Larry ran a swanky club for celebrities until he got his own Hollywood break. Sometimes, Goddard played in Larry's club for fun, and also helped him out in other ways over the years.

But for the moment, Goddard was entranced. When he was a kid, he'd watched Kitty Kallen on Perry Como's TV show and fell in love with her voice. He never dreamed he would hear anything of the sort again. But there, on the stage before him, stood a young woman whose voice made Goddard tremble.

***

"Hey, you okay?" Maureen asked, rubbing Goddard's shoulder.

Startled, he sipped the brandy in his hand and glanced at the piano where the woman was finishing her song. "She's got talent."

Maureen clasped her hands in front of her. "Yup, she used to sing in USO shows. She's the star of the Savannah Valley Chorale."

"Very good. Are you in this musical group?" he asked. So they had a chorale group. Interesting . . .

"Me? No. I can't carry a tune to save my life." She folded her arms, a defensive posture people used when they felt insecure, Goddard had learned. "I write detective novels and let the extroverts have their fun."

He nodded. "There's music in writing you know. Words have rhythm and songs have words. I can't remember what we call them," he joked.

"Are you talking about lyrics, Mr. Sampson?" Maureen teased, letting her hands drop to her sides.

"Ah, yes, I think I am." He took a bigger sip of his brandy.

Maureen waved for the woman seated at the piano to join them. She clenched her jaw and gave one of those determined smiles that let you know there's an important person you need to meet. The woman stood, covered the piano keys, grabbed her refreshments, and started walking over.

"Mary, meet Mr. Goddard Sampson. This is only his second day at Savannah Valley. Isn't this penthouse breathtaking?" Maureen chattered. "In case you don't already know, he's a retired composer and conductor." She folded her arms again. "He plays piano too."

Mary made the last few steps before offering Goddard her hand. "Mr. Sampson, it's lovely to meet you. I'm familiar with your work; I don't know who wouldn't be. You're a musical genius." She giggled and then touched her lips, looking embarrassed.

Goddard nodded with upturned lips. Not a full smile, but enough to acknowledge and accept the compliment. "That was quite the performance, Mary. Maureen tells me you did USO shows. Whatever brought you here?"

"Long story, but the short version is, I didn't expect to ever get married, so I created a magazine about how to live your best life no matter your marital status or age. That was a good three decades ago. Then, surprise, surprise, I met the love of my life at age thirty-eight, got married, and we had a daughter. So when a large publisher offered to buy me out, I was all for it. Sadly, my husband died two years ago. But on a happier note, my daughter is expecting a baby in a few weeks! Anyway, Savannah Valley is gorgeous, has everything, and I can still travel if I want. But it's nice to sit back and enjoy life. There's so much to do here."

"Like starting and directing the chorale I was telling Goddard about," Maureen said.

"Oh, yes. Well, I've always loved singing. It was fun to travel the world, backpack through Europe, and sing in everything from cabarets to small stages. The last performances I did were for the soldiers, two tours worth." She sipped her cola and pinched off a piece of cheese. "After the last one, none of the men made it home. That's when I decided to hang up my hat and count my blessings. I still think about all the young men and women who didn't make it." Her eyes glassed over.

"Ms. Mary, people like you made a bad situation a little more bearable ," Goddard said. "It sounds like you had a wild side, backpacking and cabarets." In spite of himself, he felt a show tune growing in his gut, a result of the mere mention of entertaining and the war.

Mary blushed. "Thank you. I guess you're around my age. Safe to assume you experienced the war firsthand?"

Goddard nodded. An uncomfortable silence wrapped around the three neighbors.

Maureen searched the crowd for Sydney, met her eyes, and gave her a 'Come save me' look. Sydney hurried over.

"Goddard, Mary, Maureen—how did I go so long without finding you?" she said, kissing each of them on the cheek. "Mary, I always enjoy your performances. Did you tell Goddard about the chorale?" She turned to him. "You simply must come to one of our rehearsals. We're all in it, except for Maureen, but we're working on her." Sydney gave Maureen's arm a playful nudge.

"I don't sing," Maureen reminded her.

Goddard pursed his lips. "Maybe I will come."

"Great!" Sydney and Mary said together, laughing and clapping their hands.

"Linda!" Sydney called. "Come."

Linda hiked her white, sequined evening gown and hurried over. "What's going on? Did I miss something?" She raised double eyebrows.

"Goddard is going to come to our next rehearsal," Sydney enthused.

Goddard blinked. Once again, he wondered what he was getting into.

"It's tomorrow at 5 p.m. in the arts center. There's an auditorium with a stage and piano," Sydney informed him.

Linda scrunched her shoulders in excitement and

squeezed one eye closed as she let her angst take over. "Do you think . . . can we talk you into playing something for us? For the group tomorrow, I mean. We don't have an accompanist and we would be so honored if you could play just a small thing."

Mary's mouth dropped open. She moved to cover it with the back of her hand, and the cheese wedge and crackers slid to the floor. "Oh dear, I was too excited." She stooped , picked up the bits, and stood upright in a rush. "Please, Mr. Sampson."

"I . . . " Goddard stammered. The women stared at him with wide eyes. "Okay." At this rate, the only way I'll rest is when I'm dead, he thought.

Maureen smirked. "Guess we'll see you tomorrow at five then." She grabbed Sydney's arm and led her off, leaving Goddard to talk with Linda and Mary. "Can you believe we're going to have *the* Goddard Sampson playing for us? Yay!"

Gordan couldn't help but overhear their animated voices as the women turned away.

"Shhh, we sound like a couple of star struck schoolgirls," Sydney reprimanded Maureen and herself.

"Composure is not something to be lost in this crowd."

Goddard glanced toward the two women, noting that Maureen squared her shoulders and lifted her chin, in an obvious effort to appear nonchalant, as they both blended with the crowd. A waiter walked past with a tray of margaritas, and he took one. "Would you ladies care for one?"

"No, thank you," Mary said. "I'm afraid drinking isn't my thing anymore. It hits me too hard. I'm stuck with soft drinks now."

"I'll take one," Linda said, accepting the salt-rimmed cocktail. "Seriously, Mr. Sampson, we really do appreciate your willingness to put up with us. I know a bunch of singing silver foxes wasn't on your agenda for tomorrow, but I promise you won't regret it."

Goddard nodded graciously. "I never regret taking an opportunity to share the joy of music, dear Linda. After all, it's my passion."

Mary turned to Goddard. "Would you mind if I sang one more number? I do miss performing."

Goddard looked at the piano, winked at Linda, and motioned to Mary. "Shall I audition for tomorrow? I do hope I'll be good enough."

Linda and Mary gasped.

"Do you know Autumn Leaves?" he asked.

Mary nodded, "I do." She bowed her head for him to go first and then followed him to the piano.

When Goddard sat, the room turned to him in anticipation. Mary took her station by the side of the piano, and the guests gathered in a half circle around the baby grand. Goddard set the pace with a highly ornamented introduction. The jazz tune was slow and Mary's voice was deep. The soothing tones mellowed the party and signaled that the evening was drawing to an end.

Light applause enveloped Mary and Goddard as their faces reflected the joy they felt in that shared moment, the kind of moment only those who perform can understand. A kindred high, where music captivates the mind, bringing forth memories of past performances, final bows, and drawn curtains. It echoed in their chests and coursed through their veins.

The guests drifted from the room into the waiting elevator. Goddard knew they were leaving the party with the song on their minds and in their hearts, thinking of days gone by. The beauty of music was that it meant something different to each listener. Music was an art. And art was personal.

The caterers packed their supplies and cleaned the rooms. When they finally left, Goddard poured a finger of his special brandy and set it on top of the baby grand. He played several variations on the theme in Autumn Leaves before closing the lid.

Then he carried his brandy into the bedroom and addressed the urn on the window ledge. "Well, Alice, I guess this is your way of telling me my curtain is not closed and I still have an encore left. Thank you, darling."

CHAPTER FIVE

he sun's golden rays illuminated Goddard's bedroom, warming the air-conditioned space.

He disliked room-darkening shades, preferring to rise with the sun as his alarm clock. He shifted higher on the pillows to get a glimpse of the rolling hills in the distance. From that angle, the golf course and lake were hidden. Blue skies called to him.

He dressed quickly, eager to get outside and take in the tranquility he was so desperate to experience. Just him, enjoying an early-morning stroll, then relaxing on the patio of the golf course café, sipping Earl Grey tea with honey and cream. He rushed onto the elevator.

The elevator doors opened to the lobby, and Goddard saw a handful of people sprinkled throughout the space. He took the side exit toward the golf club, his hands in his pockets, and his step a bit slower. The outdoors was his muse.

The club was abuzz with early-morning golfers. Goddard headed to the patio where a handful of tables were occupied, all by people he didn't know. Splendid, he thought. He chose a table with a large umbrella to shade him from the sun's direct rays. He pushed his sunglasses onto his head, pulled his reading glasses from his shirt pocket, and perused the menu on the table.

"Good morning, sir," the waitress said. Her black uniform was neat and pressed. "Have you had a chance to look over the menu yet?"

He squinted up at her over his glasses. "Yes, I'll have an Earl Grey with cream and honey, a chocolate croissant, and the fruit cup."

"Sounds delicious, I'll be right back with your tea." The waitress retreated with a warm smile.

Goddard traded his reading glasses for sunglasses, sat back, took a deep, cleansing breath, and let it out in a rush. He felt refreshed and at peace, but it didn't last long. He heard a commotion inside the building and, looking through the window, saw three large men. Several wait staff were fluttering around them.

The waitress returned with Goddard's tea. "Are you Mr. Sampson?"

Before he could reply, a bellowing voice penetrated Goddard's soul. "Keys! There you are."

Goddard gasped. He'd invited Larry to brunch before he left LA, but he never dreamed his friend would show up this soon, and with no warning.

The large man made his way to where Goddard sat, head in hands. "You could have waited for me, you know. Geez, I flew out here last night. Thought I'd get here early and found out you beat me to it" Two security guards sat at an adjoining table and crossed their arms over their chests. Larry sank into a chair, leaned back, stretched out his long legs, and looked around. "Nice place."

The stunned-looking waitress was still by the table. Goddard glanced at her and tipped his head toward his friend. "He'll have coffee, black. Give him a minute to scan the menu, though."

"Certainly," she said, scurrying inside to the coffee station.

"Bored yet, Keys?" Larry quipped.

A golf cart putted by with two women chatting in the back. A caddy drove while they sipped from metal water bottles. Goddard looked at the cart with interest. Maybe he should get one and drive into the woods for some solitude. Finally, he answered Larry's question. "Not yet."

"Damn, I won't lie. I came out here with high hopes of bringing you back to LA. I got the green light to produce that movie."

Goddard resettled in his chair. The last time Larry had sought his talents, he'd ended up a musical superstar with twelve awards from four countries. No question, he was grateful. But he'd worked hard for forty years and it was time to retire. He'd put away all his unfinished compositions, given a farewell performance, and sub- mitted to a flurry of interviews. As far as show biz was concerned, he was yesterday's news, and that's how he wanted it. That's also how the business worked. Once the going fad was over, the fan base dwindled. Without fans, including producers and directors, a composer was history.

"I'm retired," Goddard insisted. He stirred a squeeze of honey and splash of cream into his tea. "I'm washed up, yesterday's news."

"On the contrary," Larry said, settling back in his chair. "Your style is one of kind, my friend." The waitress returned with Goddard's order and Larry's coffee. "Thank you, I'll have oatmeal with extra raisins, no sugar, a side of milk, and butter," Larry said.

"Of course, I'll put that order in for you now." She left through the glass door.

"You've been eating that breakfast since I met you," Goddard observed.

Larry nodded. "Breakfast doesn't excite me."

"Maybe it would if you tried something new."

"It got me this far in life," Larry shrugged.

"What's with the detail?" Goddard asked, pointing to the security guards.

"I wasn't sure what kind of welcome I'd face. The airport had paparazzi, but this place is tight. I like this place." Larry sipped his coffee and looked around approvingly. "Okay, I put it out there, you think about it. So, what are you up to here? Don't tell me you haven't got your feet in anything yet."

Goddard considered telling his friend about the welcome committee, his newfound friends, the cocktail party, and the promise to listen in at the chorale rehearsal. But these wouldn't strengthen his argument for retirement and against Larry's proposal.

"Goddard!" a familiar voice called from the patio door. It was masculine but not as boisterous as Larry's. Patrick stepped up to the table and extended his golf-gloved hand to Larry. "Patrick, I live in Goddard's building."

Larry stood and accepted the man's hand. "Larry, old friend."

Goddard sighed inwardly. So much for tranquility. "Morning, Patrick. Pull up a chair."

"Maybe for a few, I want to get on the course." Patrick chose a chair facing the fairway.

"Patrick's wife, Sydney, and a few others, put together a welcome committee for me." Goddard skirted around the details.

"They also talked him into meeting us for dinner and throwing a cocktail party in his penthouse. And tonight, he's agreed to listen to the community chorus," Patrick informed Larry in the name of friendly banter. Goddard closed his eyes, bit a melon ball, and decided to just go with the flow.

"Really, the chorus is quite good," Patrick said.

"Well, well, well." Larry slapped his thigh. "Seems like you've been busy in your retirement, Keys."

Goddard sighed, "Larry and I are war buddies. He calls me Keys because I played piano."

Patrick nodded.

The composer sipped his tea. "Seriously, Larry, I do not want to get involved in any projects. I'm tired."

Larry smirked. "Yeah, right. And I'm a hairy goat. Music's in your blood. There's no way in hell you're going to go a month without some sort of musical project under your belt. I know you."

"No, I'm done. I promised to listen, not take over." Goddard pulled off a piece of croissant and rolled it into a little dough ball. Saying the words aloud felt wrong. In some way, he looked forward to watching the chorale. Last night, playing for Mary and hearing her sing, brought back that inner joy, and caused Goddard to have the best night's rest he'd had in more than a year. His mind didn't race, appreciation filled his heart, and he was able to wake with fresh eyes.

The waitress brought Larry's breakfast, and after garnishing his oatmeal with milk, butter, and raisins, the big man dug in. "Patrick, are you a betting man?" he asked between bites.

Goddard furrowed his brow. "What are you talking about?"

Larry pulled his wallet from his back pocket, thumbed through some bills, and slid a single dollar across the table. "I have a dollar that says you'll be on a music project in a week."

"Larry, I said I do not want to get involved. I need to relax, to have no pressure, deadlines, or critics. If I get bored, I'll think about it, but I do not plan on revisiting that part of my life."

"You seemed to have a good time last night," Patrick reminded him.

Last night, Goddard had noticed Patrick in a corner with a plate of California rolls. He figured the man made himself one with the shadows to get out of mingling and having to follow Sydney around. But being on the outskirts allowed him to observe the entire room, and when Goddard played for Mary, Patrick had joined the group around the piano.

"I was taken by the way you and Mary worked together, although it was only one song," Patrick said.

"I own two pianos; I didn't say I wouldn't play them."

Larry laughed. "You can't wager because you know I'm right. You can't stay out of the business."

"Fine, a dollar." Goddard pulled out his own wallet and slid a single from his brown leather trifold. "Patrick, since you squealed on me, you can hold the wagers."

Patrick picked up the bills from the table and tucked them in his front pocket. "Great. I'll keep it honest. What do you consider a project?"

"Good question," Larry said. "Let's say anything that involves pursuing a performance." He gulped the contents of his coffee mug.

"Then it's a wager, my friend." Goddard put his hand out for Larry to shake and Larry grasped it.

"The bet is made. I look forward to hearing from you, Patrick." Larry took a business card from his shirt pocket and scribbled his personal cell number on the back. "Call me Friday and give me a report. I'll be out of the country for the earlier part of the week."

"Will do." Patrick took the card and stuck it in the same pocket as the two, one-dollar bills.

Goddard laughed and sipped his tea. He and Larry had wagered throughout their friendship. The bets were in fun and never led to harm or hurt feelings, and they were careful only to wager on each other and never an outside party. With the handshake over, the men went back to their breakfasts, and Patrick excused himself to take advantage of the open tee time.

Larry left when his oatmeal was finished, his security guards trailing behind. The real purpose of his visit was to get Goddard signed on for the soundtrack of his new movie. People in their industry rarely retired. They loved the business and it became their life. Larry could badger and bet all he wanted, but Goddard was adamant about retiring from show business. He left a generous tip for the waitress and headed back home.

As he walked, he observed the bustling Savannah Valley community, where pets played an important role. The roads and sidewalks were alive with women walking small dogs or riding in chunky metal bicycles with baskets sturdy enough to carry their pets. He reached the lake and sat on a bench watching the ducks inhabiting the small center island. He thought about what Larry had proposed. Some people might take Larry's wager as a challenge, but Goddard wasn't interested or even amused. He felt ready to rest. But who knew what the future might bring? If his musical calling wasn't over, then he'd pursue it again full throttle.

Back at the condos, Goddard rode up the elevator with Maureen, who was on her way to visit Sydney. They exchanged hellos and comments about the weather. Then Maureen tucked her hair behind her ear and asked, "Still planning on coming tonight?"

Goddard nodded. "Yes, I am. In fact, I'm looking forward to it." He winked.

Maureen blushed. The elevator dinged for the second floor. "Then I guess I'll see you this evening. Have a good afternoon." She stepped off and waved until the doors closed.

Goddard glanced at his watch. He had over five hours until the rehearsal. What was he going to do with that much time? Relaxing was new to him. Damn Larry, he thought. Just like him to plant these seeds of boredom.

When he reached his floor, he strode into the salon and plopped on the bench of the grand piano. His fingers found the familiar keys, and he began to play a random tune. Not a real song, he thought, his composing days were over. Or were they?

CHAPTER SIX

oddard stood outside the double oak doors of the theater. Muffled laughter and excited high-pitched voices rose hairs on his arms. A wave of heat flashed through him. He took a deep, steadying breath before opening the door.

He saw a black stage with a black backdrop dappled with sequined figures. A group of people hovered around the ebony grand piano at center stage, and several observers sat in the audience. Goddard looked for Maureen, Sydney, and Linda but didn't see them.

He remembered Maureen saying she came to the rehearsals to offer support but did not take part. So when he glimpsed a white derby hat bobbing in and out of view between the raked auditorium seats, he guessed it was her. Somehow, she seemed like the derby type. It fit her cheery, Holly Golightly personality. As he approached, the hat's owner popped up. It was Maureen.

She beamed and waved. Then she straightened her derby and sidled down the row of folded seats to the aisle. Her hazel eyes and mauve lips were muted in the auditorium lighting. "Goddard! Stay there, I'll come to you."

Goddard nodded and continued toward the end of her row.

At Maureen's call to Goddard, the commotion onstage stopped, and awe-filled murmurs took its place. The singers' reaction told Goddard that they hadn't believed his welcome committee. He smiled to himself and thought, *my* welcome committee? How presumptuous. They welcomed everyone to the building, didn't they? On the other hand, he doubted if all newcomers had soirees and were invited to sit at their dining table. In spite of himself, he felt pleased. He'd awoken that morning with a purpose, a promise to fulfill, and a rehearsal to attend. And . . . he was excited.

A stout woman wearing a yellow dress with embroidered cornflowers and white lace trim made her way to Maureen. Goddard thought Maureen's hat would have gone well with the dress, but he liked it better on Maureen.

"Maureen, aren't you going to introduce me to our guest?" the woman said. She reached for Goddard to take her hand. "I'm Dorothy."

Maureen bit her lip. "Goddard, this is Dorothy Williams. Dorothy, this is *the* Goddard Sampson."

Goddard took Dorothy's hand and bowed his head. "It is a pleasure, Ms. Williams." He noticed the absence of jewelry from the woman's hands and erred on the side of caution. It was the reason he still wore his own gold band. He didn't feel that death parted him from his wife; it only caused them a momentary pause. They would meet again, so in his mind, he was still married. If that made him a hopeless romantic, so be it.

In any case, people didn't pry when you still wore a wedding ring. Once you got to be his age, Goddard noticed people stopped respecting your personal space and asked questions like, "Are you widowed? Is there a special someone in your life?" Goddard's answer was always, "Yes, to both."

Since his wife's death, Goddard had spent many nights brooding, sipping brandy by gas-lit fires, sitting on the piano bench, with the white keys reflecting the orange dancing light. He remembered one night in particular . . .

***

It was his first night alone in the cozy New York penthouse. Alice-Katherine had loved batik accent pillows on cream-colored couches and gleaming hardwood floors. She collected throws from around the world. He pulled a folded quilt from the stand in front of the floor-to-ceiling window and studied the Amish Wedding Ring pattern with pale yellow and cornflower blue rings. It was a wedding gift from his in-laws and the piece that started the collection. The white background was still pristine, the creases the same as the day his wife folded it.

"It's too pretty to use," she had told him, smoothing the wrinkles to the edges as she draped the quilt on the wooden rack. Regardless of fame, money, and elegant sur-roundings, that quilt followed them. It was a reminder of where they started and who they were. No amount of fame and fortune would change them.

He wrapped the quilt around his shoulders and rubbed it against his face. His tears wet the unmarred fab-ric. Goddard gulped the brandy and poured his heart into the unbroken rings—the forever bond.

A year later, he sold the penthouse, had everything but his pianos and the quilt put in storage, and avoided warm and cozy. He went for rich tones and gold trims, décor that didn't remind him of Alice-Katherine, that kept him from feeling the loss. The quilt on its wooden rack with tear-stained splotches now rested in the center of the second walk-in closet, the one he would never use, the one that should have been hers at Savannah Valley.

***

"Goddard?" Maureen called, her voice sounding far away. She placed her hand on his forearm.

He blinked and shook his head. "Sorry, I got lost in thought for a moment." Then he smiled. "That is a beau-tiful dress, Ms. Williams. And Maureen, I love your hat. It suits you.

Both women blushed and thanked him.

Maureen patted his arm with a lone finger. "Breakfast,

MAESTRO | 75

tomorrow at my house," she whispered. "No talking required."

Goddard thought about declining, but the invitation lightened his gut. The darkness lifted a smidge and he nodded.

The rest of the women in the chorus, along with three men, made their way to where Goddard, Maureen, and Dorothy stood. Mary squeezed her way through the crowd. The double doors clanged closed with another round of singers. The thirty or so had doubled in minutes.

Goddard turned to Mary. "I'll be honest, this isn't what I pictured when you said 'chorale,'" Goddard confessed.

Mary reached for Goddard's hands, and out of habit, he reached for hers, too. She kissed the air beside his cheek. "I was worried you'd changed your mind." She squeezed his hands and let them slide through hers as she stepped back in the crowd. "Mr. Sampson, would you be so kind as to settle a debate for us?"

Goddard stared at her warily. "I suppose." Experience had taught him that these kinds of questions were loaded. But judging from the raised voices upon his arrival, it was going to be a professional question. That he could deal with. "What seems to be the debate?"

Mary started. "Well, it seems that some of us want to ensure our delicate voices are preserved through structured, disciplined practice."

Dorothy chimed in. "But others of us realize we aren't professional singers and don't want to endure ridiculous hours of wasted time. We don't see the point in trilling our tongues and saying our vowels. Some of us have, quite literally, been singing for three-quarters of a century. We know how to carry a tune and string a bunch of words together. We've founded businesses and performed on television, radio, and stage. We've travelled the world, and we don't want to be put in a high school chorus room. Ridiculous." She folded her arms across her chest.

Maureen raised her eyebrows and glanced first at Goddard and then Mary.

A woman from the back chimed in. "But proper warm-ups and practices save vocal chords. How can we expect to put on our show next week if we're continuously in disagreement?"

A man from the new group of arrivals spoke up. "This is why I almost didn't come today. Always the bickering. Hand out the folders and just let us sing. I don't see why we need to entertain the same battle time and again. What's the point?"

Dorothy smirked, "Exactly. We're here to sing, we're not aiming to travel the globe looking for fame and glory. No offense, Mr. Sampson. But seriously, I'm not here to learn, I just want to have fun."

"Performing with no direction leads to embarrassment,"

Mary hissed. "I won't be the laughingstock of Savannah Valley. This isn't some nonsense affair. Our audience members are distinguished people who've traveled the globe watching the best performers. I won't dare open my mouth on that stage if we don't get some sort of cohesive program. We can't even agree on warm-ups or songs, and we promised the owners we'd perform for the summer solstice. That's next Friday, in case you aren't aware. Today is Wednesday.

To Goddard's chagrin, the two women talked over each other, anger scorching the air between them. Several women tugged on Dorothy's arms. Linda squeezed Mary's shoulder in support. Then an air horn sounded. Sydney was standing on the stage with the air horn app on her cellphone blaring through the microphone.

"People, people!" she called. The group ceased talking and turned to her. "I'm appalled. We have a legend in our midst and you resort to schoolyard behavior?" She furrowed her brow. "Goddard, I'm truly sorry. This is not what I wanted to bring you into."

Mary closed her eyes and sighed. "I, too, apologize. Let's just get to the music. Dorothy?

"Agreed," the other woman said, and the two headed for the stage.

The rest of the singers followed, grumbling as they arranged themselves in straight rows on the aluminum risers, leaving the men to stand on the floor stage left.

Why so few men?" Goddard asked Maureen.

She shrugged. "Not a lot of them want to leave the golf course for choir practice." Goddard nodded. Women always outnumbered men in amateur performances, be it community chorales or theater.

On stage, Linda wheeled out a cart stacked with black leather folders. She handed them out, and the microphones amplified the sound of papers shuffling, as the singers flipped through the pieces.

Battle Hymn of the Republic, Mary called. The papers shuffled again. When all the singers were settled, she clapped four times and bounced her hand to show the singers the beat. "One, two, three, four . . ."

Goddard unfolded a seat and sat down, eyes wide. He rested his elbow on the armrest and cradled his cheek. *What have I gotten myself into?* he sighed to himself.

Maureen removed her hat and unfolded the seat beside him. "May I?"

He glanced at her, "Of course." He returned his eyes to the stage. The man who'd arrived with the last group of singers closed his folder. He was dressed in khakis and a maroon sport coat and used a lion's head cane to maneuver his way to center stage. Goddard hadn't noticed the cane before. A faded scar stretched diagonally across his face, accentuated by the harsh stage lights.

Mary found Goddard and Maureen in the audience

and smiled. Then she turned back to the waiting singers. "Bill, will you give us a starting note?"

Goddard focused on the man named Bill.

Bill hummed and the chorale followed. Some singers closed their eyes and others tilted their heads to focus on the tone.

After the humming stopped, Mary started again. "One, two, three, four. . ."

"I thought she said they were singing show tunes," Goddard whispered to Maureen.

"They will," she affirmed. "But they focused on this one because Bill wanted it, and all the ladies loved it." She faced Goddard. "They really are hard working. Don't let the bickering get to you."

Goddard nodded. He knew all too well the kind of bickering that went on in the performing arts, although he supposed it happened in other professions, too. It was the job of the director, conductor, or supervisor to lead people from the depths of disorder into the realm of success. He watched Mary bounce her hand, not quite in time.

Bill's solemn voice floated from the stage. "Mine, eyes have seen the glory . . ." He held the last syllable of "glory" for two heartbeats before a slight crescendo into "of the coming of the Lord." Goddard sat straighter in his seat. Bill closed his eyes and folded his hands over the top of the cane and pulled back, a tender diminuendo.

When it was time for the chorus, the other two men stepped forward beside Bill and joined him in an emotional "Glory, glory, hallelujah." The altos, lower female voices, joined in with "The truth is marching on" and continued to hum harmony with the men. Goddard shifted in his seat; tears wet his lashes. Bill continued his solo until the next chorus, where the sopranos joined in a rousing "Glory, glory, hallelujah." In the following verses, the chorale hummed in harmony while Bill sang the melody. At the final "The truth is marching on," Goddard stood. Maureen followed. Goddard felt tears gleam in his eyes.

Maureen clapped and Goddard joined her, but with more restraint. Goddard rose from his seat and headed toward the stairs, stage right. He tucked his hands in his pockets as he jogged up the steps. When he reached the stage, he addressed the three men: "It's moments like this that remind me why life is worth living. I came here today to hear a rehearsal. What I heard instead was music from the soul, the kind of music only mature generations truly appreciate. No matter your purpose, your warm-up, or your intentions, your goal is to tell your story."

He pointed to Bill. "Whether you close your eyes and deliver the haunting message or clasp your cane to belt out the chorus, you perform from your heart." He faced the other men. "When you come to join him, you are members of a troop. I have no doubt the three of you have served in some capacity, and that bond is reflected in your music and extends to the audience."

The women in the choir shifted.

Goddard stood back to address them. "I watched each and every one of you. Your eyes, your breaths, the tears dripping over your cheeks. You've been touched by war, and this song arose from your endurance, strength, and empathy. You were shaped by that experience and came together, all of you." He spread his arms to encompass every member of the chorale. "This . . . you have blown me away. Thank you."

Bill approached Goddard, hand outstretched. "No, thank *you*, sir."

Goddard nodded and clasped Bill's hand. Then the other men came forward to shake his hand, and several of the women, including Mary.

Goddard stepped back. "I would be honored to be your accompanist for other pieces, but this song is best acapella. I cannot and will not improve on perfection."

Bill's eyes reddened, and Mary gasped and covered her mouth with her hand.

Sydney climbed down from the alto section. "I don't care how old we are or how we got here, to receive such high praise from you gave me goosebumps, and I'm not alone. Those of us who had successful careers, especially us self-made types, rarely received enough praise for our efforts. For me, Goddard, those words are worth more than gold."

Several of the members clapped and it was contagious. They applauded Goddard, and he felt embarrassed. In his mind, he hadn't even done anything. A woman from the back row called to Mary, "Can we rehearse again tomorrow? We only have eight days and then it's showtime."

Goddard nodded to Mary, and she affirmed with a joy-filled, "It looks like a yes!"

Sydney and Linda went to Goddard. "We have music if you want to look it over. Please have dinner with us again tonight. We can do a more low-key bite, in town."

"I'd like that," Goddard nodded. "Now, let me hear what else we're bringing to the residents of Savannah Valley." And with that small bit of praise, the plus-or-minus sixty singers took their places and tackled four more numbers. They were good, but not Battle Hymn of the Republic good. Tomorrow is another day, Goddard thought.

Today, he'd observed their inner fire, what burned in their souls. He needed to capture that emotion, shake it up, and pop the cork. The question was, how? The pieces they had were adequate , but he wanted to bring something new to the show, a theme, a finale. The word fire repeated in his mind. Would they accept it? Could they handle it?

Maureen patted his arm. "You have a menacing look on your face. Care to share?"

Goddard gave a mysterious smile. "Ever play with fire?"

CHAPTER SEVEN

Pizza for Piazza

he elevator was stalled at the second floor, and Goddard held the door open while Patrick ran back to his condo for Sydney's "furred ball of treasure." They were meeting Maureen and Linda in the lobby and then heading into town for a quick bite. The sun would be up for another hour and not a cloud marred the sky.

"It's perfect for Piazza," Sydney said. "You don't mind, do you Goddard? I know the others won't." Goddard shook his head no, and he and Sydney waited in the elevator while Patrick retrieved said treasure. When he returned, Piazza was tucked into a large, mauve purse that matched her Italian leather collar.

Goddard released the door and the elevator finished its descent. When they stepped off, he noticed how the lights in the lobby reflected off the dog's white coat, making it shine. "I finally meet the little ball of fur," he said, patting the petite, pear-shaped head with its single top knot. "You're a cute little thing, aren't you? What kind of dog is he, or is it a she?" Goddard asked."

"A she, and she's a Maltese," Sydney said, kissing the dog's tiny head.

Patrick hoisted the purse strap over his shoulder. Goddard thought the man looked rather silly holding a purse with a dog's head peeping out. On the other hand, the mauve contrasted nicely with his black polo, tan khakis, and black Salvatore Ferragamo loafers, which he wore without socks. Patrick had grown on Goddard over the past few days. The man had a way about him that was a lot like Larry but more subdued. Like Larry, his new friend played golf by day and wasn't afraid to dig into a hunk of meat at dinner. Goddard, on the other hand, enjoyed long, solitary walks and rarely ate red meat. When he was younger, he'd enjoyed biking and hikes in the mountains, where he could sit on the top of the world, dreaming of new adventures. He recalled one hike long ago . . .

***

Goddard sat on the edge of a cliff, along the Appalachian trail, swinging his legs. He marveled at the expanse below him, but since returning to the United States after touring Europe, the beauty of nature kept reminding him of blaring brass and striking strings. At that moment, *The Ride of the Valkyries* by Richard Wagner played itself through in his head.

He'd seen the *Ring* cycle live at The Royal College of Music in Stockholm, and it had opened his eyes to the world of music and symbolism and the compassion, empathy, and excellence required of a true master of the art. Compassion allowed him to feel the melodies swell and subside like the waves of an internal ocean. Empathy let him imagine how others would receive his works. And excellence? That was required on his part, or the enjoyment would be lost. He imagined families coming to experience the music he created and memories being made and shared.

As Goddard sat watching the distant clouds stalled over the valley, he thought: *It is well-known that music is the foundation for speech, the stitching that mends a heart weeping from the woes of life. It brought communities together, with local musicians performing for their neighbors and people young and old dusting off the instruments in their attics. It brought the rich and poor together in a shared moment.*

He pulled his feet beneath him and headed back to the trail and down the mountain. Soon after, he would leave New York, and launch his career, putting his passion out for the world as a composer, conductor, and teacher.

***

Patrick's voice brought Goddard back to the present. "Goddard, you want to sit between the ladies or between me and the door?" he asked , now holding the purse under his arm, Piazza's head poking out.

The composer smiled. "Sounds like a loaded question."

Patrick laughed, "Fine, me and the door it is. Sorry, ladies."

Maureen and Linda had joined them in the lobby. Goddard cherished his memories, but he now felt himself getting wrapped in the warm blanket of new faces, new friends, and a new family of sorts. To his surprise, he liked it.

Once they were settled in the community limo, Patrick handed Piazza to Sydney. She moved the fluffy dog from the purse to her lap. She'd swapped her usual luxury attire for a pink polo shirt and olive-green chinos. Maureen was wearing a violet sundress and matching shawl, while Linda had donned a pale blue blouse with matching scarf and white slacks. Goddard felt overdressed in his white button-up shirt, navy blazer, and tan slacks.

Fifteen minutes later, the limo stopped and let them out next to a white-and-gold sign announcing Savannah Towne Square. They entered the square through a green metal arch. It had the historic charm of many old town centers: cobblestone streets, black streetlamps, and ornate building facades. Sydney tucked her head through the strap of Piazza's carrier so she could carry it diagonally and relieve some of the weight the small dog added to her shoulder.

"Little thing's a heavy sucker," she said.

"Aww, that little thing?" Linda cooed. "She's just adorable." She scratched Piazza between the eyes with a single French-manicured nail. The dog pressed into the cooing woman's touch. "My heart gets all aflutter every time I see her."

Sydney kissed the Maltese's head again, and the dog squinted and blinked when her hair grazed its eyes. The dog mom pulled a tissue from a side pouch in the purse and dabbed the dog's tears. "Are we still in agreement for pizza?"

"I am," Patrick affirmed. "What about you, Goddard? You eat pizza?"

"I'm from New York," Goddard said , "Pizza is in my blood."

"Then pizza it is," Linda announced. "This place takes me back to living on Arthur Avenue in the Bronx."

"I've never been there, but I've heard it has the best Italian food outside of Italy," Maureen said.

Patrick stepped between Linda and Maureen. "When you eat here, it's like eating on Arthur Avenue—or Italy. The owner's a friend of mine. Lives in the community. We meet up on the golf course a few times a week."

Sydney fell in step beside Goddard. "John owned an Italian restaurant on Arthur Avenue and sold it a few years ago. His sauce is amazing."

Goddard nodded. Pizza had been a big part of his life when he traveled. "So, does Piazza eat pizza?"

Sydney bumped his arm. "John makes a tiny one for her. Brown rice dough and red sauce with shredded cheddar. She loves it."

"Gourmet dog pizza. I love it," Maureen chuckled. "Actually, it's pretty bland. Needs more salt," Patrick confessed.

"You tried the dog's pizza ?" Goddard asked, keeping his shock in check.

"He'll try anything, if you tell him it's food," Sydney teased.

"I've never had an adventurous palette," Maureen admitted.

"Enough wine and it doesn't matter," Linda laughed.

They chose to dine al fresco at a black wrought-iron table beneath a red umbrella. The matching chairs were made comfortable with red cushions, and a wine list sat atop the red-checked tablecloth. Goddard noticed a metal loop welded to all the chair bottoms, apparently for dog leashes. Nice touch, he thought.

Sydney took Piazza from the purse, pulled a thin leash from a side pouch, and attached it to her wide-eyed pooch's collar. She slipped the Swarovski crystal-studded handle over her wrist and set the dog in her lap.

Piazza studied Goddard with her black-button eyes, and he couldn't help smiling back. "She's quite small, isn't she? Is she a pup?" He pursed his lips at the innocent face.

Sydney picked the dog up and made kissing noises beside the shining black nose. "Not quite a year, they figure. She's a whopping four pounds. Probably won't get much bigger."

Goddard removed his silverware from the red, rolled napkin and placed it on the table. He folded the napkin into a triangle and draped it over his thigh. The women watched him.

Patrick pulled the silverware from his napkin, straightened it out, folded it in half, and tucked it in his lap.

The three women laughed. "What do you do with your napkin?" Maureen asked Linda and Sydney.

Linda unrolled hers and folded it like Goddard. "Huh, I guess I'm a triangle person."

Maureen unfurled hers with a snap and tucked it under the neckline of her dress while the others looked on in surprise. "Just kidding!" she laughed, pulling the napkin out and folding it over once before placing it on her lap.

Sydney readjusted Piazza, unrolled her napkin, and folded it into a square. "I usually do a trifold, but with Piazza on my lap, I'll keep my napkin on the table."

"Isn't it funny, we all left our silverware in the same spot," Maureen pointed out. "I love detail. I put a lot of it in my books, because it makes reading that much more interesting. Plus, dining tells a lot about a person."

"Speaking of which—our waiter is coming," Patrick announced. "Any requests before he gets here?"

"I have no preference," Goddard said.

"Two pies, one meat lovers' and the other veggie?" Patrick asked the women.

"Sounds good to me," Linda said. "Do they have oysters on the half?"

"Oh, they do," Sydney answered.

Maureen stuck her tongue between her teeth. "Unless it's sushi, I want my fish cooked. Let's get those for all of you, and I'll have a shrimp cocktail."

"You really do like shrimp, don't you?" Goddard said.

Maureen blushed. "I guess I do. Good thing I'm not a flamingo, I'd turn pink."

Linda snorted. "You already are, darlin'."

Maureen frowned at her, blushing even more.

The waiter took their orders and left. Linda settled back and crossed her legs. "Sydney, why don't you tell the story about how you got Piazza?" She raised her eyebrows at Goddard and Maureen. "You won't believe what they went through. I mean, they actually acquired an apartment in Milan."

The waiter returned with a bottle of Cappellano Otin Fiorin Pie` Rupestris. "Compliments of the owner." He removed the cork and let the bottle breathe in a bucket of ice. Then he pressed the button on a timer in his apron pocket and motioned for the waitress to bring the water carafe. Another waitress carried the glasses. "I will return. If you need me, my name is Carl." The man slipped through the doors and disappeared behind the darkened glass.

Sydney waited for the waitresses to leave and settled

into her seat, smoothing Piazza's fur. "Well, as I'm sure you know, Rome, Italy, is home to Piazza Navona."

Goddard nodded and sipped his water. "I know it quite well, actually."

She smiled at him. So, we were strolling through, taking in the fountain and such, when I saw a little white blur dash past us. Everyone knows there are stray dogs all over the piazzas, but this dog was so small, I had to follow it. We wound up jogging to this wall-like divider, with grass and plants growing down the center. The poor little thing ran behind a plant and hid."

"The poor baby," Maureen whispered.

"I know, right?" Sydney agreed. "I tried to get close to her, but she growled. That's when Patrick took out a piece of bread he'd tucked in his bag from our lunch. She popped her nose in the air and sniffed. He tossed the piece to her, and she swallowed it without even bothering to chew. It tore at my heart, the little starved thing. After that, she let us pick her up, and we took her to the animal clinic. They checked her over and directed us to a shelter outside the city. They made us leave her there until we could provide the required documentation and answer an insane number of questions. Don't get me wrong, I want to see the strays go to loving homes, but I swear, it was more complicated than adopting a baby!"

Patrick lifted the little fluff ball from Sydney's lap

onto his. "That's when we decided to rent an apartment and extend our stay. We found out that when you want to adopt a dog in Italy, you have to fill out a questionnaire, have a home visit, get asked the same questions in person, and still have another questionnaire to ensure your information was accurate."

"We had to provide our birth certificates, intentions for when we left Rome, New York home information, and then some," Sydney continued. Finally, we hired an attorney to take care of the paperwork and finalize the adoption. It was easier getting her into the United States and having her quarantined than it was to get her out of Italy. " Sydney cradled the dog's chin. "I wouldn't have changed a thing. She's a love and worth every step."

"She's the lucky one," Linda said. "Look at her now, living in the lap of luxury."

The waiter came back and poured the wine in Patrick's glass, then stood by and waited for his approval. "Delicious," he said. "Please give John our thanks." Then the waiter poured wine for the rest of the table.

Linda held her wineglass at her lips. "So, do you speak Italian to her? She mustn't speak . . . oh my gosh, is that even how you would say it?"

Maureen took a sip from her glass. "I think you mean, is she bilingual? I'm sure it's no different than teaching them a new trick. Sydney?"

Sydney glanced at Patrick. "We kind of like being the only ones who know her secret. We wanted to make the transition easy on her, so we talk to her in Italian. She knows most basic commands, so there isn't any real effort on her part or ours."

Goddard bent toward the white fluff on Patrick's lap. "Bella ragazza, non sei fortunata?" Piazza peered at him, then settled her head back on Patrick's leg. She knew she was a lucky girl. "I'll tell you, Italy was a love affair. The baroque fountains, Casa Verde, the Teatro Alla Scalla—the list is endless. Such a beautiful country. I loved the architecture and art," Goddard enthused.

The waiter returned with Piazza's dinner, and the waitresses followed with the oysters and Maureen's shrimp cocktail. "Is there anything else I can get for you?" the waiter asked.

"No, thank you," Linda said.

The waiter bowed his head and left, gesturing for the waitresses to follow him.

"I wonder if they're in training?" Maureen asked.

"No, John just likes to treat his customers well. Back on Arthur Avenue, he served family style. This is a new venture in an area that wouldn't necessarily welcome an Italian restaurant." Patrick took an oyster, scooped a spoon of cocktail sauce, and dabbed it on the clean, shucked treat. "Goddard, you should try these, they're fantastic."

"Thank you." Goddard took one, squeezed a lemon wedge over it, and slurped it from the shell. He unfolded his triangular napkin and replaced it with the used portion still hidden in the folds.

Sydney took Piazza from Patrick and hooked her leash on the metal loop created for that purpose. Once on the sidewalk, the little dog began to dance. First, she went up on her hind legs, then she twirled, her mauve leash wrapping itself around her middle. Her mother unwrapped the leash, and then picked up the dog plate with the canine culinary creation cut into bite-sized pieces fit for the Thumbelina of dogs.

"Siediti," Sydney said, pointing to the sidewalk. Piazza sat and remained seated until Sydney placed the plate on the pavement, pointed to it, and said, "Brava."

Goddard studied the dog and the people around the table. The warm, Savannah sun mingled with the warmth of the wine. He settled back in his chair, crossed his legs, and swirled the wine. The waiter brought the pizzas, one in each hand. The waitress put out two racks and the man slid the pizzas into place. A second waitress held a stack of plates, while the waiter served. Goddard and Patrick opted for the meat lovers, while the women went with the veggie lovers, although Sydney stole a bite of Patrick's.

The dog lay on the sidewalk, licking her impossibly small paws. She spotted Goddard watching her and jumped on his shin. "May I?" he asked.

"Of course," Sydney said. "I think she likes you."

Goddard lifted the tiny creature into his lap. Her black-marble eyes searched his own. "Grazie, piccolina," he said.

CHAPTER EIGHT

Breakfast at Maureen's

he sun beat through Goddard's ninth-floor penthouse windows. He opened his eyes on cue. It was his routine in California, then New York, and now in Savannah Valley. The cleaning service's vacuum whirred in the next room. Goddard had ordered the daily package with weekly detailing, all part of the Savannah Flat's extras.

"Siri, play Verdi's *La Traviata*," he called. The opera held a special place in Goddard's life; it was the first he conducted while in Italy. The violins overtook the hustle and bustle of the cleaning crew.

Dressed in the tank top and boxers he slept in, Goddard wandered to his walk-in closet. He pulled a monogrammed dress shirt off the hanger, then decided against it and hung it back up. From his dresser, he grabbed a pair of white socks with black treble clefs embroidered on them and tossed them on the dressing chair. The opera's music lilted along, and then it caught him. He grabbed a yellow-striped bow tie, clutched it in his right hand, and stood in front of the full-length mirror in the mahogany-trimmed closet, conducting an invisible orchestra, hands bouncing to the violins and woodwinds, humming along with the vocals.

Goddard swept the bow tie up and pulled his left hand back to hush the strings. Then an upsweep of the tie signaled the precise moment the melody took over in the pit orchestra. Again, he pushed back the orchestra volume with a gentle wave of his hand, for the soprano was not to be overpowered. He spun around and held the tie as if it were a champagne flute. Then he walked back into the bedroom.

"Good morning, Goddard," Maureen said.

Goddard dropped the tie and stared at her. Then peered over her shoulder to the open bedroom door. "Morning, Maureen."

Maureen's lips twitched. "The cleaning crew let me in. Breakfast? I'm on the second floor," she deadpanned.

"Very well," Goddard agreed, matching her straight face.

"Good." Maureen made a slow turn and walked to the bedroom door with her hands tight by her sides. She paused in the threshold and peeked back at Goddard. He fluttered his fingers. The two stared at each other for a long moment, while the Vivaldi chorus roared over the Cabasse speakers. Then Maureen covered her mouth and hurried out of the room.

Thirty minutes later, Goddard rode the elevator down to Maureen's floor. He'd made certain to take his time dressing and getting ready for their breakfast. The striped bow tie lay in an empty drawer, exiled from his wardrobe. He wanted no reminder of the humiliating incident earlier.

The elevator dinged and the door opened. He sighed in frustration. He'd forgotten to ask Maureen which door was hers." There were three doors, all with gold trim. He stepped up to the first door, pressed the call button, and looked in the camera.

"Goddard?" "Hold on a second, I'll be right there," Linda's voice sang out.

The man rubbed his palms on his slacks.

Linda opened the door, her hair swept in a loose bun. She had on yoga pants, a tie-dyed sweatshirt, and white Keds. "I wasn't expecting to see you this morning. How are you?"

"Fine, fine. I'm meeting Maureen for breakfast and forgot to ask her which door." He looked down the hall toward the other two doors.

"She's on the far side," she said, pointing. "Want me to walk you there? It's no problem." She put her hands on her hips and stretched one leg, then the other. "I need my steps anyway."

"I think I'll find it. Thank you." Goddard stuck his hands in his pockets and turned to the long hallway.

"Okay, well, have a nice time," Linda said, retreating into her condo.

Goddard trudged to the end of the hall. When he reached Maureen's door, he straightened his posture. Before he could press the call button, the door opened.

"Linda called," Maureen said.

"Ah." Talk about a grapevine, Goddard thought.

"No bow tie? I'm disappointed," Maureen teased. Goddard felt his cheeks get warm. "Well, it certainly makes for interesting conversation." he said, feeling his pulse rising.

Maureen's eyes danced and she laughed. "I've yet to meet a musician who has not entertained. Come in, come in. I wasn't sure if you were a coffee or tea man, so I waited." She opened the door wider and motioned for him to enter.

Goddard stepped through, careful not to brush against Maureen, who hadn't opened the door far enough to provide comfort. The moment he entered, he was gripped by the modern décor.

The condo was a stark contrast to his penthouse. The open floor plan provided an unobstructed view of the rolling hills and lake. The sun reflected off the white-marble floors and polished wood furniture in white birch, bamboo, and pecan. There were built-in bookcases with complete sets bound in leather and one glass case he assumed contained first editions. Cream-colored sofas were scattered with gold, brown, and burgundy decorative pillows. At each end of the sofas, hand-woven baskets contained folded throws , with brown Steiff teddy bears posed on top.

"Which are you?" Maureen said, closing the door behind her. "Tea or coffee?"

"Tea."

"I have an assortment; what would you like?"

"Earl Grey or whatever." While Maureen fetched the tea, Goddard toured the living room. He noticed a mask collection on the wall above a gas fireplace. The hearth was marble as well, a continuation of the floor. The faux logs were encased in glass doors with gold trim. "These are beautiful," Goddard said, pointing to the masks.

Maureen appeared beside him. "Thank you; they're Native American. My mother was raised on a reservation where they made these masks for ceremonies. She said they were part of our ancestry. I keep them here, so I have a piece of my family with me."

"That's lovely," Goddard whispered. "About this morning . . ."

She handed him his tea. "Shh. I promise not to tell. But it was nice to see that the always-serious Goddard Sampson has a fun side. Don't shy away from getting lost in something you love. This is your life. Every single day is a gift. What you do with it is up to you." She sipped her own mug of tea. "I, for one, love dancing around to any music that strikes my fancy."

Goddard sipped his tea and then turned to face her. "That's quite insightful."

Maureen sat on one of the cream sofas and gestured for Goddard to sit opposite her. She set her tea and saucer on a glass-topped, bamboo coffee table and clutched one of the throw pillows. "Goddard, why did you retire?"

He sighed. He looked at the tea and studied the color while he searched for an answer. "I see things differently now. When I was young, I traveled to Milan, Paris, Moscow, Sydney . . . I performed all over the world. That was it. Until one night, that is."

"Hold that thought," Maureen said. She went into the kitchen and returned with a tray of mini croissants, Danish, and fresh, bite-sized fruit bits on wooden picks. "So, back to your story. Was this when you met Alice-Katherine?"

He nodded.

"She became your world."

Goddard nodded again. "Larry offered me a gig at his nightclub in Los Angeles. One thing led to another, and I wound up performing for a movie soundtrack. Then I wrote one. It was an instant hit. I continued working in Hollywood until she passed." He took a grape and rolled it in his cheek. "I regret not retiring sooner. Always working, creating, not giving her the time she deserved."

"Did she ever tell you she was unhappy?" Maureen asked.

"No, she always claimed to be happy. She had a smile that lit up a room, cliché as it may be. I can still picture her, pure white hair blowing in the breeze from a balcony in Greece, overlooking the Mediterranean. She looked like a goddess." He blinked away tears.

"It's okay to say it, Goddard. Have you?"

"What are you asking me?"

"Have you said the words, 'I miss her?'"

He shook his head. "Not to anyone but myself. After Alice-Katherine passed, I put away all my music and holed up in New York. I moved here because I wanted peace, but now I wonder if she sent me here for a second chance." He gulped the tea. "Sounds ridiculous."

"Not at all. Why do you think I invited you here? It took a long time for me to get over my husband. I still miss him, but I'm living. The people I've met here are like me. They understand fears, loss, watching your youth slip away and not knowing when it happened. You're part of that circle now. I think of Sydney, Patrick, and Linda as my new family. How long will I have them? I don't know, but they're special, because they made me realize it's okay to be happy."

Goddard sank into the line of pillows. "I don't know. Maybe it's too soon, but I feel the same way. I want to put on a performance. I want to go to that rehearsal and light the stage with a fire that will make the singers and the audience know they're not at a recital. They're in Savannah

Valley, where people have hidden talents that need to be shared."

Maureen tossed her pillow aside, grabbed a croissant and bit into it. "Bravo! Then do it."

CHAPTER NINE

Rehearsal

That night, Goddard arrived at the auditorium an hour before the rehearsal. He studied the layout and view of the stage from the last row on the right and on the left. Then he did the same from the balcony. After the chorale arrived, he would revisit those spots to assess the acoustics. He wanted to bring the stage to life. It was what he did best.

Conducting an orchestra or leading a choir meant retrieving recessed emotions from the audience. He was an artist, a man who knew how to elicit an emotional response with small, often-unnoticed tweaks. Of course, by the time he retired, he'd gone full out with visuals, historical connotations, and romance. Music was life.

Goddard climbed the stairs to the stage and sat at the ebony Yamaha grand piano. He did a flourishing introduction and laid into his own version of "Battle Hymn of the Republic." Definitely needs a snare, he decided, wondering if there was a drummer in their midst. He sat back on the bench and plucked out the melody to a piece he thought they might open with or else use as a segue from the one strong piece they knew. He asked himself: Should they sing two hymns and four show tunes? And what is the story? What was Mary trying to tell?"

Goddard remembered that Mary played in USO shows, but she didn't put them together. It was clear she loved performing, but how much of the decision making did she do ? Back then, probably none. So directing was new for her. How can I turn this into a story? he asked himself again.

The light on the stage seemed to brighten. An idea formed, and Goddard's eyes lit with a newfound enthusiasm. It was more than enthusiasm; his heart raced. Thoughts flooded his mind: holograms, a backdrop, birth of a generation, war and hope, bright lights, freedom. Out loud he declared, "The program will work!"

Goddard pulled out his cell and dialed the only number he'd thought he would need at Savannah Valley, the one to the lobby desk at Savannah Flats condos. Before the third ring, a young man answered.

"Good afternoon, this is Christopher speaking, how may I be of service?"

"Christopher, this is Goddard Sampson, from the ninth floor."

"Yes, Mr. Sampson, how may I help you?"

"I was promised any service I required would be met. I'm putting it to the test now, Christopher. I'm calling from the theater at the arts center. I need a full stage crew—lights, design, ice sculpting. Whatever you can send. The sooner the better. We have a show in less than two weeks."

Christopher paused, "Uh, will do, Mr. Sampson. But . . ."

"I know you don't know who to call, but you'll figure it out. I have faith in you."

"Thank you, Mr. Sampson. I'll get right on it."

Goddard ended the call. He played through the introductions of all six numbers. He did the same with the last lines of the same pieces. One brought attention and ended with a finale. The second made a statement. How can I piece them together between Broadway tunes? Goddard wondered. Then he got it—a trip through the decades! He pulled a small notepad from his jacket pocket and jotted down his thoughts.

Keeping his thoughts straight by writing them down wasn't a function of age; he'd always done it. He was a man of ideas, always thinking, planning, organizing, and creating. He visualized scenes, heard melodies and harmonies, and then developed stories. He often felt overwhelmed until he put it all on paper. Once he did that, a brand new idea would emerge. It was a never-ending cycle.

After the banter with the women at last night's rehearsal, he knew the best way to appease them both was to compromise. They would *perform* the warmup and open with "Dona Nobis Pacem." Immediately after that, he would have Mary and Dorothy step forward on opposite sides of the stage.

"Yes," he said aloud again, thumping the top of the piano for emphasis. Rehearsal time neared, and Goddard's excitement grew. He'd ask their permission, make sure they were on board, and then they'd have a show. He glanced at his watch: a quarter to five. It was someone's dinnertime somewhere, but at his age, he could eat after he unfurled his plan. A lamb chop didn't hold the excitement of a four-part harmony with stellar intonation, and the message that would remain. He could drink that in. No, he could absorb it through his pores.

The back doors opened, and the first wave of singers entered the auditorium. To Goddard's delight, Patrick, Sydney, Linda, Maureen, and Mary arrived together. Patrick rummaged in his pocket, pulled out Larry's business card, and waved it at Goddard. His smile stretched from ear to ear, almost lighting up the theater.

Goddard smiled back and shrugged. "You win some, you lose some." He sat back down at the piano and played a full chromatic scale. First up, slow and steady. On the descent, he quickened the pace, an accelerando. The women and Patrick watched and listened from the front row. Music is a language. You just have to have something to say, he thought.

More singers filed in. He noticed the stragglers from the day before had found the motivation to show up early. Goddard played double-octave scales, covering the circle of fifths. He then broke off into left-handed chord progressions with right-handed scales. The singers all sat in the auditorium, expecting, watching. He repeated the exercise with right-handed chord progressions.

There was a microphone on the piano. Goddard slid the button on and adjusted the height. He continued to play scales with various chords, including blues and jazz style, skipping, and overhand while he spoke. "Good evening, everyone. I trust you all came ready, willing, and able?"

The singers mumbled in agreement.

He changed the rhythm yet again. This time it was a 1-and-a-2-and-a pattern. "I always liked this one; it's fun," he said. He played a double octave and then the one note beyond. "Oops," he winked. "I always do that. Best not to make the lower keys jealous." He did the same pattern down the scale and stopped before hitting the extra note. He physically struggled to keep from pressing the key. His finger grazed the surface, but not enough to make a sound. His hand twisted with each try. He grabbed his left hand with his right and created an altercation that brought the audience into a roar of laughter. The vaudeville-like act lightened the mood and he struck the key.

Goddard knew the secret to working with top talent was reminding them they weren't above having fun. No composer wanted a symphony orchestra filled with animosity. The conductor was in control. At least, they should be, he thought.

"You know," he said in the microphone, "I only have two hands, and I need your help in a three-part round. I'm asking you all to come up here and stand on the risers. Anywhere is fine; if you have a spot you like, mark it, name it, but don't take it home with you, because I think it might cause a snit with the owners." He raised his eyebrows.

The singers laughed. Patrick, Bill, and the two other men shook their heads. All the singers made their way to the stage. It took a good five minutes for them to get situated. Maureen and Patrick remained in the audience.

"Ms. Maureen, since you don't have a job, would you mind being my page turner?"

Maureen glanced at Patrick, who urged her to go up on the stage. She climbed the stairs, arms rigid, and she stood next to the piano. She stared out at the empty seats and Patrick.

"See, now we've done it. Poor Patrick is down there all alone. Patrick, would you come up here, so we don't feel so sorry for you? Maureen, would you bring a chair from the back to the curtains for him?"

Maureen grinned and then scurried to the back to

pull a folding chair along the wooden floor to the heavy black house curtain at the front of the stage. Patrick walked up to the stage, sat in the chair, crossed his legs, and then crossed his arms over his chest. Goddard went back to his scales, adding more ornamentation and using the full range of the keyboard. The volume was a steady mezzo piano. "Maureen, take a seat by me on the bench. These pages always get the best of me." She sat beside him, squinting at the empty music rest above the keyboard. He winked and turned to the singers. "Now, I'm going to play you a melody, and just to make sure you know it, I'll sing it first. I'm a terrible singer, so you'll have to forgive me." He ended the scales on the high end of the piano, started an introduction on A below middle C, and sang, "dona, nobis, pacem." He stopped singing but continued to play just the melody with two hands. "Think you can remember that?"

The group nodded and mumbled.

"Great. Now, just to be sure, I want to hear all the men in the group. I'll sing with you. Patrick, are you in?"

Patrick nodded.

"Great!" Goddard played in a lower, singable key and led the men to sing the first part. "Okay, now altos, let's see if you can do them one better, but don't drown them out. Let's give it a try first." He played "dona, nobis, pacem" and sang with the altos. "Amazing. I just love this piece. You know what? Men, I want you to change it up a bit, like this." He sang the beginning verse the same way as when they had sung with him, then resung the same words, altering the melodic structure to create the harmony in two parts.

"Ladies, let's give this a try. Men, you start first. Altos, when they're done, you come in. Oh heck, sopranos, after the altos, you can just sing the same thing. Ready?" He didn't wait for an answer but went into the canon of "Dona Nobis Pacem." After the men reached the end of the second part, Goddard played with a noticeable crescendo and sang with them through the third part. As each group reached the end note, he squinted an eye to keep them from stopping. The first round was rough as he expected, but the second and third were perfect. He finished with a cadence and nodded for the group to release their chord.

"This song is called "Dona Nobis Pacem," he said. "It's a real musical work that I'm sure most of you have heard or even performed at some point in your life. It was written in the sixteenth or seventeenth century; the composer is still unknown. Be it Palestrina or Mozart, the fact remains: It is brilliance in its simplest form."

The group shifted. Dorothy put her hand on her hip. "Is this your way of proving that we need to warm up?"

"If that's what you take from this exercise, then wonderful," Goddard said. "I simply wanted to see if you could all follow directions."

Dorothy opened her mouth, then closed it. She shook her head and glanced at Mary who smirked at her.

Goddard went back to playing a series of memorized etudes at mezzo piano. "Tell me, anyone, what do you want from this show? If I understand correctly, it's the first here at Savannah Valley."

Bill stepped forward. "I want to be a part of something. I used to sing, before I became involved with my company, and flying to close deals and finalize contracts became my life."

Goddard nodded.

Dorothy raised her hand. "Ditto that."

Ten or twenty voices swept through the risers. "Me, too!"

"And what do you want from me? Yesterday, you asked me to come back. Today, you need to decide if it's what you want." He stopped playing, folded his hands in his lap, and crossed his ankles.

A soft murmur went through the women, and the men shifted on their feet. Bill glanced at Mary, Dorothy unfurrowed her brows, and several women whispered back and forth. Sydney sighed and glanced at Linda. She raised her hand and Goddard nodded in encouragement.

Sydney lifted her chin, "I want to be a part of anything you create. I'm a huge fan, and this is the greatest honor I can achieve in the years I have left."

Linda raised her hand next. "I've never performed. I grew up on a dairy farm, raised my siblings, and sang in church. It was the closest I ever got." She shrugged, "This exercise sounded amazing. If you can do that in ten minutes, I want to see what you can do with us by next Friday. I want your friendship and experience."

"May I go next?" Dorothy asked.

"Of course,"Goddard said.

"I never took music seriously until I joined this chorale. It was just something to pass the time. But you remind me of Liberace. I apologize for yesterday. Sydney is right, just being on stage with you is a huge honor."

"Mary," Goddard said, "I am asking for your permission to bring this show to life. If you say yes, then I need to know that the rest of you are committed to making this one hell of a show for the residents and their families. I'm going to take a walk while you discuss it." He looked at his watch. "I'll be back in ten minutes. No hard feelings either way; this is your group and your show. I'm the outsider here." Goddard stood, stepped down off the stage, and walked up the center aisle. At the halfway point, he turned back to the chorus and bowed before leaving the auditorium.

CHAPTER 10

he men's room was a short distance from the double doors of the auditorium. Goddard decided to stroll down there and sit in the lounge area. There was no performance, so the room would have little foot traffic. Even if it was only ten minutes, he would relish the silence. He was halfway there when a young man in a pressed black uniform rushed through the revolving doors, panting.

"Are you Mr. Goddard Sampson?"

Goddard smiled. He could say no and get away with it.

"I'm Christopher." He paused long enough to clasp his thighs and catch his breath. "Please, excuse me, sir. I ran here from the condos."

"Whatever did you run for?" Goddard asked.

"You said you wanted the stage crew as soon as possible. So I called my buddy who does sets and tech work for one of the local theater companies. Actually, I'm one of their light guys." He inhaled deeply through his nose. "The rest of the crew can be here for tomorrow's rehearsal. Is that soon enough?"

Goddard blinked at him. "Splendid! I knew you'd come through for me."

Christopher grinned and nodded. "We're excited to work with you, Mr. Sampson. I'm not sure exactly what you need, but I told Jimmy—that's my friend—I'd get more details from you. That way, we'll be ready to set up tomorrow." He pulled a small pad and a pen from his pocket. I'm ready."

"I'll be honest, I'm surprised—no, delighted. Thank you, Christopher," Goddard said. "Just give me a minute to collect my thoughts."

Goddard's head was spinning. Everything was coming together.

He stepped back against the wall, his mind focused on a vision. It was how he created the masterpieces for which he was so well known. His shows drew huge audiences, no matter what country hosted his visit. His venues included castle ruins, mansions, cruise ships, amphitheaters, and the most notable stages on the globe. He'd conducted as many philharmonic orchestras as the years he'd been alive—maybe more—Goddard realized, with some surprise, that he was just as excited about creating a masterpiece for his new friends at Savannah Valley. Perhaps, he still had more to give. He turned to Christopher and said, "Okay. Let's start with my wildest hopes and see if you and your crew can make them come to fruition."

Christopher poised his pen to take notes. "We have toys to make it happen, Mr. Sampson. Just tell me what you're looking for."

"I want fire."

The young man nodded and scribbled.

Goddard continued. "We're starting this program with a sunrise in the background. I want an evening sky giving way to morning light, as the singers build their crescendo. By the end of the first song, we'll transition with a train whistle and—do we have steam train capabilities?"

"No problem, and I assume you want mist as well?" Christopher asked.

"Let's hold off on actual smoke. Asthma and COPD are only two of the health issues that come to mind with this group," Goddard shared.

"We can dim the lights."

Goddard tapped his chin. "Can you give me a New York City skyline or marquee lighting above the chorale?"

"I think we can. We'll play around with it and let you see the result before the end of tomorrow's rehearsal."

"Good, good. Safe to assume you can give me a silhouette on the back? Moon rise, river shine, and a burst of flames?"

Christopher perked up. His smile proved he understood Goddard's vision.

They continued to make plans and discuss possibilities until Sydney opened the door of the auditorium. "Goddard, we're ready for you now." She pushed the door open wider for him to step through.

He turned to Christopher, who was busy writing notes. "I need to finish this rehearsal, but I'll be back at the penthouse by eight o'clock. Can we continue then?"

"Sure thing, Mr. Sampson," Christopher said, giving Goddard a thumbs up as he hurried out the door.

As Goddard walked back into the auditorium, he saw Dorothy standing in the aisle in front of Sydney. She had her hands folded in front of her. "I apologize if I came off as rude."

Goddard smiled and clasped her hands. "Does this mean we're all ready to put this show into motion?"

Several members of the chorale nodded. Sydney and Linda clapped their hands and jogged to the stage. Mary followed them, calling, "Come everyone, let's show Mr. Sampson what we've got." The singers assembled on the risers in single-file lines. First the top, then the middle, and last the bottom. The men were still on the left. Goddard knew they'd been hard at work while he was outside. Mary took her place, raised her hands, and the group set into the warm-up Goddard had left them with.

Goddard took to the balcony to assess the acoustics. The group went right into "Moon River," and as he reached the doors, he heard a soft voice singing along. It reminded him of Audrey Hepburn, a whisper from the dark back corner of the balcony. Experience taught him to temper his reaction. Gushing waves of praise would have an adverse effect. Instead, he would sit back and appreciate this unrealized talent, give the singer time and space, avoid confrontation, assess the person and situation.

He took a seat in the balcony, center aisle, back row. He wanted to hear the harmony on stage, but also the whispered solo from the shadows. He imagined his friend Larry's reaction. He'd be in that corner talking her up, telling her she belonged in pictures, the old fool.

Goddard made his way to the front of the balcony as the chorale eased into the end of, "Moon River" and switched their music for the next piece. He called down: "I want everyone to do that again, but this time I'll join you." He made his way up the aisle to the double door and stopped. "I'd be delighted if you'd join us, Maureen. I'll save you a space on my piano bench." He winked at the shadowed figure and left her to contemplate the next move.

***

Goddard arrived at the auditorium the next evening to find a van parked outside and Christopher in the lobby.

"I promised you the crew today," Christopher said, gesturing toward the door. "Like I said, I'm one of the lighting guys. The rest of the crew are outside."

Goddard rubbed his hands together. "Splendid! I can't wait to get to work."

"We also brought a portfolio of past ice sculptures. The artist is on his way. He's excited to work with you, Mr. Sampson."

Goddard nodded. "We have about ten minutes until the others . . ." He was interrupted by a burst of crew members wheeling large cases.

"Your lighting experts," Christopher explained. "And this is my friend, Jimmy, who's in charge." Goddard shook hands with a bearded young man dressed in jeans and a denim shirt.

"Thank you all," Goddard said, turning to the crew as they stood waiting for directions. "I appreciate all of you. Let's see if you can make my wildest hopes become a reality."

The crew created a semi-circle around Goddard. "Chris told us what you want, and we have the means to make it happen, Mr. Sampson," Jimmy said. "I wish our other clients pushed us to the limits like you have. We're thrilled you've given us this opportunity."

"To start with, I want fire," Goddard said.

The lead man nodded and then consulted a piece of paper taped to one of the cases. "And an evening sky, sunrise, and a train whistle, correct? But no mist. Plus, a New York skyline and marquee lighting."

Goddard nodded back.

"Shouldn't be a problem," Jimmy said. "We'll play

around and see what we come up with by the end of your rehearsal."

"Good, good. And you can give me a silhouette on the backdrop: moon rise, river shine, and flames?" Goddard asked.

The crew looked excited. Murmurs spread through the seven men and three women. A middle-aged man in a flannel shirt tucked into a pair of jeans walked into the lobby. He saw the smiling crew and caught their excitement. His lips tugged upward at the corners and he raised his eyebrows.

"This show is going to be awesome, Dude," Christopher told the man who Goddard assumed was the sculptor.

The man nodded to Goddard. "Jacob—I'll be creating your ice work."

"Thank you, Jacob. We'll talk in a bit. I want to find out what can be done." Goddard regarded the crew before him as essential for delivering the best for Savannah Valley. "I'm going to need costuming, holograms, a snare drum . . ."

"I was a percussionist in the Marine Corps Band." A female crew member stood, back straight, hair pulled into a tight ponytail.

"Can you spare her?" Goddard asked Jimmy.

He shrugged, "Sure."

They continued to make plans and discuss possibilities

until the choir members began to arrive. Once they were all inside the two sets of auditorium doors, the crew filed in with their equipment. Then they went behind the curtains with their headsets and flashlights.

The choir began to rehearse, and before long, lights they didn't know were above them brought their singing to life.

During a break, Sydney and Patrick handed out Savannah Valley water bottles to the singers and crew. Jacob waited at the stage for Goddard, holding an open sketch pad. When the composer approached him, he met him halfway.

"I believe I captured your vision, Mr. Sampson. Here are two for you to choose from." He handed the book to Goddard, who studied the sketches. "If you don't like these, I'll . . ."

Goddard raised his palm. "No, I like them, but the bottom one really speaks to me. It has an underlying beauty that sets it apart. We'll go with that one; after all, are we not here to celebrate creativity, no matter which manner or mastermind?" He winked at the sculptor.

"I like you, Mr. Sampson. Ice sculpting isn't what most people think of when you say art."

"Do people enjoy it?" Goddard asked.

"Yes," Jacob answered.

"Then it *is* art." He patted the artist on the shoulder. "Are you married, Jacob?"

"Yes, my wife's pregnant, and this job will pay for the matching crib and dresser set she wants." The man laughed.

"Is that so?" Goddard said. "Well then, invite her to the concert. See me when you deliver the sculpture and I'll give you two tickets."

Jacob grinned. "Thank you, Mr. Sampson. I know she's going to love this." The man closed his sketch pad and headed up the aisle with a spring in his step that wasn't there before.

The singers took their places again, and the crew dimmed the lights. Overhead, imitation stars twinkled against the black curtains and ceiling. Murmurs of "This is pretty" and "Wow" rustled through the choir, capturing how Goddard felt the first night Bill stepped forward to sing, and when he heard Maureen singing in the balcony. He returned to the stage, sat at the piano, and started a piece they'd never heard, as blue flames overtook the darkened backdrop.

CHAPTER 11

"*L*arry called to check in on the bet," Patrick informed Goddard.

He expected his friend would. "He's all about winning, but not for the money. Pure, unadulterated bragging rights make Larry tick." He took a putter from his bag at the back of the golf cart and strode toward the little ball on the manicured green. He'd finally taken Patrick up on his offer to play a round of golf. The men had a lunch reservation at the golf club for two o'clock and figured they'd play until then. "You sure you want to put up with me this long?" Goddard joked.

"Nine holes, eighteen, doesn't matter to me," Patrick said. "I just like being outside in the sun and not having to look over charts and stats or worry about bottom lines. Believe it or not, I had cataract surgery that changed my life. I can't believe how beautiful the colors are. You miss a lot and don't even realize it." He scanned the green and squinted at the cloudless sky, his Cartier sunglasses snug on the bridge of his nose. "Sydney's over the moon about the concert tomorrow. Don't think I've seen her that excited in years."

I'm glad. There's nothing like performing to raise the adrenaline. It keeps you young." Goddard tapped the ball and it rolled into the hole. "Well, look at that."

Patrick recorded the score in his phone. "This golf app is the best invention ever. Remember having to use those little pencils and trying to write in the boxes in the burning sun?"

Goddard laughed, "I do."

Patrick crouched on the ground and lined up his putt. "Syd can't understand how I can come out here every day. To tell you the truth, I don't have an answer. No game is the same, and the weather changes with the hands on the clock. He stood, gave the ball a gentle tap, and it dropped into the hole.

"I guess that's what relaxing is all about. Finding something that takes you away." Goddard leaned against the back of the cart while Patrick scooped up his ball.

Bzzzz. The phone rang in Patrick's pocket. He tucked the club under his arm, pulled off his glove, and answered, "Patrick." He nodded while the voice on the other end spoke. "Hey, Larry. Yeah, he's right here." He glanced at Goddard. "Uh huh. Yup. Okay then." He ended the call and stuck the phone back in his pocket.

"Are you going to keep me in suspense ?" Goddard asked.

"Oh, you'll know soon enough," Patrick laughed. He

slid the putter into his bag just as a procession of golf carts cruised up to where he and Goddard stood. "Yup, and there you have it."

Goddard turned to see the entourage behind Larry, lost his balance, and caught himself on the headlight. "What the hell is this?" he called to the man behind the steering wheel of the lead cart.

"It's your coming out of retirement debut. Smile for the camera!" Larry stopped the cart, climbed out, and pulled three cigars from his pocket. He kept one and handed the others to Goddard and Patrick. "Welcome back!"

"I am not *back*." Goddard put the cigar in his shirt pocket.

Three young women and one young man dressed in casual attire, with press passes dangling from their necks, rode in the second golf cart, with Larry's security detail in cart number three. A tall woman reporter stepped forward, holding her phone out to Goddard to record his response. "Is it true, you're coming out of retirement?"

Another woman did the same, "What made you change your mind, Mr. Sampson?"

The man clicked pictures of Goddard, Larry, and Patrick.

"Don't go getting me involved in this," Patrick huffed. "Do I look like I'm ready for my close-up?"

Goddard leaned against the golf cart, hands on the

hood. "What are you doing, Larry? Do you think this will make me take on your soundtrack? Is that it? Don't you think a straightforward phone call, asking for my help, would get you further?"

Larry lit his cigar and took a puff. "Nope."

Patrick laughed. "This has got to be the best thing I've witnessed here." He tucked his cigar in his shirt pocket. "Are you staying for the show tomorrow, Larry?"

Goddard hissed at Patrick. "Why did you say that?"

"I wouldn't miss it," Larry patted Goddard's shoulder. "Already bought my tickets."

"Tickets? More than one?" Goddard asked.

"Yup, what's a performance without a media presence?" Larry grinned and slapped Goddard on the back. "Don't disappoint." The man climbed back in his golf cart. The reporters finished recording the conversation and then took pictures of everything in their view. Larry started the cart and drove away laughing. The media carts followed with Larry's security detail bringing up the rear.

After Larry left, Goddard and Patrick decided to cut short their morning game. They arrived for their lunch reservation early, only to find the reporters sitting at one of the patio tables. Patrick tugged Goddard's arm. "Come on, we can eat inside," he said.

Goddard sighed. "No, there's no reason to ruin the whole day. Let's eat outside and just ignore them." He chose a table on the other side of the patio and sat with his back to the reporters.

Patrick sat across from him. "Are you sure?" he said.

"Yeah, let them have their pictures, it's nothing new." Then he studied the menu. "I've been looking forward to the duck foie gras and pear tatin."

Patrick looked over Goddard's shoulder as one of the women at the media table stepped toward them. "Mr. Sampson?"

Goddard breathed in a reply, "Yes."

"My name is Shelly, and I just want you to know that we're all huge fans."

"And you want an autograph?" Goddard took a pen from his pocket and looked for something to write on.

"Although that would be more than awesome, we just want you to know we aren't here to make a scene. Larry made it clear we were not to interfere with anyone here, and quite frankly, we don't want to be like the paparazzi who hound people. We're journalism students, and Jim is completing his master's in orchestration. We want to be taken seriously. Unless you give us the go ahead, we won't bother you. No more pictures either."

Patrick raised his eyebrows at Goddard. "Sounds sincere."

Goddard pushed his sunglasses onto his head and looked at her. The young woman didn't have a phone or notepad. "Thank you for that. Tomorrow, bring me your tickets and I'll sign them. I'll even pose for pictures with all of you."

Shelley backed toward her table, a radiant smile on her face. "Thank you, Mr. Sampson. Enjoy your lunch, and good luck tomorrow."

Back in his penthouse, Goddard sat at the piano. He plucked out a few notes and stared at the elevator. He kept expecting Larry to barge in, but the man was nowhere, not that Goddard had tried to find him. Still, he wondered: Do I really want to be left alone?"

Tonight was the dress rehearsal. Goddard had put on a black Armani suit, adding a red-sequined tie to lighten the mood. Nerves would be on edge, and excitement would be high, but not compared to tomorrow night. The familiar flutter in his chest made the question repeat in his mind. "Is it over? Is this my final performance?"

He never drank before a rehearsal or performance. He was always too keyed up, plus, the first bite of food and sip of cognac afterward tasted that much better. But after the curtains closed and the green room emptied, calm would envelop him. Then he often grabbed a midnight bite with other performers or visitors. He decided that tomorrow night, he'd have a burger with truffle fries after the show.

He leaned into a flourishing introduction and played a selection of show tunes mingled with bits from movie soundtracks. He kept his eyes closed and his heart open. The sound of the elevator buzzer broke his concentration. He stopped playing and walked to the camera, expecting to see Larry's smug face, but it was Mary.

Goddard granted her access without a word, a sinking feeling in his gut. Like most theater folk, Goddard was superstitious. Surprises on dress rehearsal night were bad omens. So when the doors opened and Mary stepped out, Goddard greeted her warmly, even though his stomach was in knots.

Mary had a large bag over her shoulder, the one she used to carry copies of her music. "I brought you this," she said, handing him the sac. "My daughter went into labor not fifteen minutes ago. It's my first grandchild. I have to go be with her." Tears rolled down her cheeks.

"I understand," Goddard reassured her, although he felt like crying himself. "It isn't the first time life has interfered with a show, and it won't be the last." Damn Larry, he thought. Of all times to show up and invite the press.

"You know I wanted this, probably more than anyone on that stage. But I'm going to be a grandma, Goddard. My daughter lives in Oregon, so I need to leave on the first flight, tonight at seven."

Goddard placed the bag of sheet music on the floor and clasped Mary's hands. "I'm happy for you, Mary. You're going to make a wonderful grandma. Don't feel guilty; just go to your daughter, because you don't get a second chance at this. The stage will be here when you get back. And if you decide to stay out there, then that's where you need to be. You're not stopping who you are, you're just changing your journey."

Mary squeezed his hands. "Thank you, Goddard."

He released his hands and handed her a mono-grammed handkerchief from his pocket. "Now, dry your tears and go. There's a tiny fan waiting to meet you."

Mary smiled through her tears. "There's a whole audience of fans waiting for you, Goddard. You can't retire from being a Maestro. As the elevator door closed, she waved his handkerchief and called, "Break a leg tomorrow night!"

An hour later, the singers filed into the auditorium's first three rows. A rack of black-satin robes stood waiting. The costume designer had made shimmering silver sashes to reflect the overhead lights and add to the stage effects. Goddard had ordered leather folders embossed with "SVC" for each singer.

He hurried to the stage and stood by the piano. "Good evening, everyone," he said, voice quiet and calm. "I trust you are all excited for tomorrow."

The group murmured, heads nodding in agreement. Then he told them about Mary, and they were stunned into silence.

Finally, Dorothy stood. "Who's going to take her place?"

Over the past week, Mary had taken the lead in singing "Moon River," with the chorale providing harmony until the song's chorus, when they sang in tutti. It balanced nicely with Bill's solo in "The Battle Hymn of the Republic. They'd worked out where Mary should stand for her solo and where Bill should stand for his. Goddard and the lead crewman, had come up with an artistic solution, using the stage lights and holograms to provide the theatrical flair Goddard was after. Now, Mary wasn't going to perform, and after all their rehearsing, the singers looked defeated. Goddard did his best to boost their confidence and morale. "Tonight, we run through the show and make sure all the kinks are out. You've all worked hard, and I'm proud of you. Mary's absence is just a hiccup. We should be happy for her new role as a grandma. She made the right decision and I stand by that." Goddard sat at the piano and played the beginning of each piece, his signal to the group that he was ready to begin.

Dorothy wouldn't let up. "But who gets the role? Are we all just going to sing it? How will that work with the stage effects?"

Goddard sighed. "It will be resolved by the intermission." He wished he felt as confident as he sounded.

Satisfied, Dorothy climbed the stage steps and took her place on the risers.

Goddard started them singing "Dona Nobis Pacem," and the canon resounded in the auditorium. He left the stage to listen from the balcony, hoping the solution to his dilemma was singing in the shadows.

CHAPTER 12

t four o'clock the next day, Goddard watched as Jacob, the ice artist, rolled up to the front entrance of the arts center. He pulled a massive, canvas-covered sculpture balanced on a wooden dolly with four casters. His assistant rode in the back to ensure the piece remained stable, and then provided the necessary muscle to get the piece over the pavement lips. Two theater attendants held the front doors open for the duo. Goddard had made sure the table was in place in the lobby before he left the night before.

Goddard watched with interest as the two strong men expertly slid the sculpture off the dolly and onto the table. Then they positioned a large drip pan underneath and attached a clear hose to the back of the sculpture to siphon the water as it melted.

"This should last a good six hours," Jacob said. "Don't worry, there won't be a flood. We'll be back after the concert to remove it."

Sydney emerged from the auditorium with Linda and waved at Jacob and his assistant. "Is the ice sculpture about to be unveiled?" Sydney asked. Then she turned to Goddard. "Patrick is home waiting for our son to arrive," she said. "He flew in for the performance. We'll probably get a bite after. You will join us, won't you?"

"I'd be delighted," Goddard said.

"I'm tagging along, too," Linda said. "Don't know where yet, but I think they're keeping Sky open, so we could just ride the elevator up after the show."

"Oh, I like the sound of that," Sydney agreed. "I feel so important. I forgot what putting yourself out there felt like."

"Well, you'll both have plenty of fans in the audience," Goddard said. "The Savannah Valley's rich widows—Edith, Glenda, Darcy, and Sharon—will be in the balcony with my friend Larry, along with your son Patrick and John, the Italian restaurant owner and his wife, who are Linda's guests," he added.

"Why do I feel so giddy?" Linda asked, fanning her face with her hand. "We've earned this night, haven't we, Goddard?"

"You absolutely have. You ladies put in your all. Working behind the scenes, scheduling deliveries, and making sure the décor was exactly what I expected. Your talents come in many forms. I want you to know how much I appreciate all you've done." Goddard smiled, then gestured to Jacob, and the artist unhooked the canvas from the sculpture.

The father-to-be stepped aside with a leather strap in his hand. His assistant stood on the other side of the sculpture. "I received a message from Edith this morning. She wants to be here for the unveiling," Jacob said.

"I'm here," Edith called from the revolving door. Her heels clicked on the granite floor. "Thanks for waiting. When I heard Jacob was the sculptor, I just had to see his masterpiece now. I couldn't wait until tonight."

Seeing the surprised looks on the others' faces, Edith laughed, filling the lobby with the echo. "I studied fine art and directing before law school. This is exactly where I want to be." She nodded to Jacob. "I think we're all here."

"Wait!" Maureen called, pushing through the door. "Sorry, I was on the phone with my editor." She turned to Edith. "This should be fabulous. Are you coming to the show tonight as well?"

"We all are," Edith assured.

"I do hope you enjoy it," Maureen said.

"Now?" Jacob asked.

Goddard nodded.

Jacob pulled the canvas from the sculpture. It was magnificent, about five feet tall. The artist had chiseled three chorale members in robes and Goddard at the piano. Flames were shaved into the ice above the singers, along with the name of the ensemble, Savannah Valley Chorale.

"Jacob, you outdid yourself," Edith enthused.

"Goddard wanted all sixty singers, but I told him even I can't work miracles," Jacob grinned.

"It's splendid," Goddard said. "Jacob, did you ask your wife about attending this evening's performance?"

"I did," Jacob affirmed.

"Wonderful." Goddard pulled out two envelopes and handed them to Jacob. "One contains the tickets for tonight's show. The other is for your wife and the nursery."

"I didn't know you were expecting. Congratulations!" Edith said. "The sculpture is perfect, thank you. Goddard, ladies, I'll see you this evening."

"Looking forward to it," Sydney called, as Edith pushed through the revolving doors.

Linda and Sydney disappeared into the auditorium, leaving Goddard and Jacob alone. His assistant had taken the dolly back to the van. Jacob put his hand out to Goddard. "Thank you for the gift. I don't know what to say."

"You getting that nursery set up is all the thanks I need," Goddard handed him a business card. "This man makes luxury furniture. Tell him what you want and I'll settle the tab. The second envelope is a note to your wife. She may feel uneasy about accepting this gift, but please tell her not to. It's my pleasure."

"Thank you, again. I can't believe it." Jacob shook Goddard's hand a second time and then went back to his refrigerated truck.

Back at his penthouse, Goddard heard the grandfather clock strike six. Dressed in a black, custom-made tux, he stepped into his elevator and pressed the button for the second floor. When the elevator stopped, Sydney and Linda ushered him to Maureen's condo.

"See you in half an hour," Linda said as she kissed his cheek.

Sydney did the same. "If you see Patrick, remind him the show starts at seven. I've said it a hundred times, but I'm nervous."

"I will," Goddard assured her.

The two women clicked back toward the elevator, in their black heels and matching black dresses.

Goddard pressed the call button on Maureen's door and stood in view of the camera. "I've come to escort you."

She opened the door, shoeless, dressed in an elegant black sheath, and holding a glass of wine. "No, you came to see if I'd changed my mind."

He stepped inside the doorway. "Have you?"

Maureen stepped back. "I don't know. These last two weeks have been amazing. Before you showed up, the chorale seemed like a hobby, a pastime. You made it real."

"I'm sorry . . ."

She pressed her hand to his chest. "No, don't apologize. You brought us all to life. Before, we were staggering our way. Tonight, they have a sold-out show."

"*We* have a sold-out show," he corrected.

Maureen looked away. "I don't know if I can do it. I'm scared."

Goddard took her hand. "Maureen, you're an accomplished woman, beloved by readers all over the world.

What is it that makes your confidence falter? You know the lines, the melody, and your voice is lovely. What is it, Maureen?" The woman's glistening hazel eyes struck something deep in Goddard's core. "Come to the theater with me. Mary's most likely a grandmother now. The chorale is backstage in the greenroom. Attendants are steaming robes while the make-up artists reduce glare with their magic brushes. Why not bring your own magic and share it with others? I know you can do this."

She pulled her hand from his. "You've performed your whole life. You don't know what it's like for me. I was the shy girl, never picked for plays, didn't join chorus or band. Instead, I sat in the library reading about faraway places. It wasn't that I didn't believe in myself as much as I didn't want to be judged."

Goddard chuckled, "You're a novelist, Maureen. Everyone who reads your books judges you, but you're used to that. I tell you what, let's head over. Larry has a seat for you in the balcony. If you change your mind, let me know before seven. When the curtains open, the show begins, no matter, your choice. But if it makes a difference, imagine the audience in their underwear. It'll be our private joke."

Maureen slipped a pair of black heels over her stockings

and grabbed her purse. Goddard opened the door and she motioned for him to go first. "Age before beauty."

"Ouch."

The two took the limo to the theater and were dropped off at the entrance to the arts center's theater doors.

"You look handsome." Maureen kissed Goddard's cheek. "Don't break a leg."

Goddard returned the kiss to her cheek, "Do you feel it? The excitement? The buzz?"

Maureen gave a tight smile. "Fine."

"Come, Ms. Maureen. Your friends await." They exited the limo and Goddard opened the side door to the theater for her to go first. "I will carry you through this, and no matter what happens, you are not alone."

The two separated and Maureen headed for the balcony. Goddard went backstage and checked on the singers, who looked elegant in their new robes. Onstage, he peeked through the curtains and glanced at the balcony and the full auditorium. Bill was warming up backstage. Through the doorway, Goddard could see the ice sculpture sparkling under the lobby lights, and Larry's entourage honoring it with a quick photo shoot.

The house lights blinked and the crowd silenced. The singers filed onstage and took their spots on the risers, behind the curtain. Goddard walked onto the stage, and applause broke out from the front row to the back. From the balcony, someone called, "Maestro!" Goddard bowed and took his seat at the piano. Then the curtains parted, revealing the chorale. The dark backdrop came to life with the first note of "Dona Nobis Pacem." The men sang, then the altos, and finally the sopranos. They crescendoed and faded away for Goddard's lead-in to "Moon River."

The spotlight dimmed, and a new circle of light appeared, searching the balcony. A quiet, gentle voice that embodied emotion filled the auditorium. Maureen stood in shadow, like the first time Goddard had heard her. But this time as she sang, she stepped into the light. It illuminated her black-robed form as she sang from the front of the balcony, the group on stage carrying her through the passage. When the song ended, a thunderous applause swept through the audience. Maureen slipped back into the shadows, and Goddard flourished his introduction to "Give My Regards to Broadway."

The chorus continued their musical journey through the decades, as Goddard had imagined, fading away at the end, with a New York skyline on the backdrop. The music stopped, and Bill slipped behind the curtain. A distant snare captivated the audience, and goosebumps spread over Goddard's arms. Bill marched onto the stage in step with the drum, played by the crewmember who'd served in the Marine Corps Band. Then silence, and the stage went black. The spotlight appeared with Bill in the center, and his voice brought tears to Goddard's eyes. He wept for untapped voices and the passion they held. He wept for Maureen and Bill and the courage it took to release their passion. He wept for all the members of the chorale who'd embraced his leadership. And he wept for himself, for the splendid opportunity to share his gift of music once more.

As the man sang, "Mine eyes have seen the glory," he walked to the front of the stage. The other men fell in behind him and sang, "Glory, glory, hallelujah." The light rose over the risers and the women appeared. The altos joined in the next chorus, followed by the sopranos. At the song's end, the snare drum beat softened, and the men held their chord. The special effect of blue flames flickered on the backdrop.

The women on the risers raised their voices in unison, and "I am fire!" resonated through the audience. The blue flames grew until they reached halfway up the curtained wall, and then those same blue lights spelled out "Savannah Valley Chorale." When the last note was sung, the stage went black. Stars twinkled overhead. The audience stood and applauded and cheered. Goddard's heart was full for the first time in years.

Larry leaned over the balcony and hollered, "Encore!"

Later, the friends gathered at Sky with Edith, Sharon, Glenda, and Darcy. Sydney and Patrick's son joined them. The waiter poured champagne for the group. Most of the other performers were scattered throughout the restaurant with their own parties. Larry had left at curtain close.

Maureen drew Goddard toward her and whispered in his ear, "Thank you."

He placed his hand over hers and said, "I'm proud of you, Maureen." Looking around the table he added, "I'm proud of all of you." Maureen raised her glass, "To us!"

"To us," the group toasted.

"Goddard, have you decided?" Maureen asked, her eyes sparkling.

"I have," he teased.

"Decided what?" Patrick implored.

Goddard smiled and winked. "You can call me 'Maestro.'"

EPILOGUE

It's never too late to start believing in yourself, or in those around you. As a business owner, and leader, it is my job to call on the right people at the right time. When I get it right, we make beautiful music together. When I get it wrong, I disappoint myself, the people I am leading, and ultimately the customers we serve. It is my job to identify opportunities to add to the success of my team. Goddard too realized this, only he did it at the young age of only 14 when he heard the potential of a woman's chorus from the streets of New York City. Offering to play for them, not for money but for the opportunity to see these ladies reach their fullest potential, he invested in their success.

The only way to ensure we as a society are successful, and produce an award winning concerto of life, is to lift up those that may not believe they are good enough. Show those we encounter throughout our day that they're vital through our words and actions. Throughout his life Goddard did this with everyone he encountered. From those he led on stage, to those in charge of the stage itself. From those in charge of the lighting, to the man asked to produce the ice sculpture the guest would experience upon entering the theater. He encouraged them to reach deep and perform at a level they themselves didn't think possible.

We all have different levels of confidence at various times in our lives. All too often leaders lean on, and invest in, those that have the talent to deliver the results they need to be successful. Instead, as leaders, what if we encouraged those that have the confidence and invested in those that don't. When we do this, we don't just get results...we create results that can be seen as a world class concerto. An ensemble of people working together for a common goal, to create something not seen (or heard) before, while lifting people to greatness along the way. Imagine if Goddard focused on just the top ⅓ musicians or choir and left out, or dismissed, the remaining ⅔? What if he treated that ⅔ as merely supporting casts or artists? Would he have achieved the level of success in his career that he did? Would he have seen the potential in Maureen, calling on her when Mary had to step down to attend the birth of her first grandchild?

What I love about Goddard is he believes that despite our self perceived skill levels, we are all unique, we are all vital. He can't stop lifting up those around him. He invests and encourages in others to rise to greatness. He took on a group of people with vastly different experiences, talents, and backgrounds. He encouraged those that needed it and invested in those that didn't believe they could.

Goddard thought retirement is where he belonged, thanks to his friend Larry, bluntly intervening in his plans,

Goddard was forced to see that he had more to give. However, this time he would focus on serving others in a more intentional manner. This time it would be about encouraging those around him to see their own potential.

I see Larry as his Angel sent by God to challenge Goddard to see his continued purpose. We all have these Angels in our lives. Sadly, most of the time we don't see them as Angels but as simply voices of encouragement from a friend or acquaintance.

I started working odd jobs for my uncles at the age of 13. Both owning their own, yet separate businesses. At 15 I was working after school, weekends, and my summer breaks for the man who would eventually become my step-father. He owned a landscape and general contracting company. In my early 20's I bought him out of the landscape side of the business, allowing him to continue to grow the general contracting side. After several years of growing that business, I found myself dealing with a life crisis that changed the course of my life. At the age of 25 I found myself working for an amazing couple in the wireless retail business. Over the next 23 years I would help them to grow their business, partner with them, and eventually buy them out. I then grew the business to over 120 retail stores nationwide.

After selling the company that I spent the last 23 years of my life investing in, I (like Goddard) thought I was done. Not exactly sure what to do with the rest of my years, I thought relaxing and enjoying life was the answer. I was wrong. I quickly realized I still had so much more to achieve. Like Goddard, a friend pulled me back into the business world. However, this time I am determined to do something to make the world a better place for my daughters, my grandchildren (when I have them) and the rest of the generations to follow. I want to do something to make a difference in people's lives. I want to encourage those that don't see themselves as vital, and to inspire those that do, to live a vital life - a life of gratitude, openness, and kindness.

Over the years I have had the honor of leading many great people. Inevitably I get asked "who was the most influential mentor you had in your life? Who guided you towards this style of leadership?" Whereas I have looked up to many leaders in my lifetime, there is only one that didn't just speak on what great leadership looks like, he showed it. He lived it out every day he was alive. Jesus Christ. Jesus lead with gratitude of those we was surrounded by. He called on and invested in those who didn't think they deserved to be. He led with openness, never judging one's actions but instead understanding their situations and inspiring them to see things differently. He led with kindness, always putting others before Himself...all the way to the cross. I see Jesus as the Maestro of maestros. Follow

His lead, and we will create a symphony worthy of His sacrifice.

Goddard is truly a maestro. He understands the importance of others in creating something great. We are all in this ensemble of life together. Looking for the good in those around us is how we live life as a beautiful symphony, instead of individual instruments playing to our own sheet music we call life.

It's mine and Stacie's hope that Goddard's fans walk away from his story challenged to look at how they can make an impact in people's lives. We hope his fans are inspired to become maestros of their own. That they give it one more try, whatever that "it" is. You still have so much to do...

It's Review Time

Please leave a review. It would mean so much to us. We want to share the possibilities of reinventing your life when you think you have nothing more to give. Who do you know needs inspiration to find joy in their life again? The more people know about this book, maybe, they too can find the *Maestro* in themselves, no matter their age.

Good or bad, we want to hear from you. All it takes is one little sentence, more is good too. We just want to know if you enjoyed this book.

https://www.amazon.com/Maestro-Songteller-Savannah-Rick-Fessler-ebook/dp/B0BBXVLDZ8/

ABOUT THE AUTHORS

RICK FESSLER

First, I am a father to my two beautiful daughters and a husband to my amazing wife. During my lifetime, I've been an accomplished entrepreneur, owning numerous companies—often at the same time. As a leader, I define my team's success or failure in terms of the moral principles that are the bedrock on which I have built my organizations—integrity, compassion, gratitude, openness, and kindness.

I am the Founder and CEO of CH&M Holdings, an umbrella over a group of faith-based, family-focused organizations. Vidl, however, is my heart's passion. It's a reminder that "You're Vital" and encourages people to "Be Vital." What began as a great idea for an everyday consumer product (a water bottle) evolved into a movement to foster human connections and to remind the world that each individual is vital–absolutely important, essential, even treasured.

https://vidllife.com/

STACIE FESSLER

I am a mother to my two beautiful daughters and a wife to my amazing husband. Before I became one of the top real estate agents in St. Louis, I was a high school English teacher with a passion for helping others. I measure my personal success by how well I'm able to help others find an innate value within themselves.

I love traveling with my family. Whether it's a trip to the beach or the mountains, these vital moments fill my heart with joy. I also enjoy playing golf and tennis, as well as quality time with my friends.

CPSIA information can be obtained
at www.ICGtesting.com
Printed in the USA
BVHW032113161022
649505BV00005B/14

9 798885 810166